D1229280

Simply BALi

A Complete Guide to a
Healthy, Whole Foods Lifestyle

Dawn Corridore & Jen Harris

Copyright ©2016 by Inner Renovo, LLC

Published and distributed in the United States.

Cover Photographer: Nicole DeCarlo/decarlophotography.com

Cover location: The Cottage Luxe Kitchen designed by Rosanne Darmanin/Cottage Luxe, Casually Elegant Design & Styling/cottageluxe.com

Inside photographs: Dawn Corridore, Jen Harris, Nicole DeCarlo/decarlophotography.com

Editors: Beth Landi, David Leone and Nicole DeCarlo.

Cover Design: Bill Herrin

Inside Design: Anjoo Fellner

BALi and BALi Eating Plan® are trademarks of PYRLess Group, LLC. These trademarks are used throughout *Simply* BALi pursuant to a license from PYRLess Group, LLC. If you are interested in a license to use the BALi name, please direct all licensing inquiries to Roby Mitchell, M.D. at drfitt@me.com with the subject line: BALi License Inquiry.

Please note the other trademarks used in this book are the property of the company, which they are associated with. BALi and BALi Eating Plan® are trademarks of PYRLess Group, LLC.

The information included in this book is for educational purposes only. *Simply* BALi has been read and approved by Roby Mitchell, M.D. It is not intended or implied to be a substitute for professional medical advice. The reader should always consult his or her healthcare provider to determine the appropriateness of the information for their own situation or if they have any questions regarding a medical condition or treatment plan. Reading the information in this book does not create a physician-patient relationship. In the event you use any of the information in this book for yourself, which is your constitutional right, the authors assume no responsibility for your actions.

All rights reserved. No part of this book may be used or reproduced in any manner whatsoever without written permission except in the case of brief quotations embodied in book reviews. For information, contact *Inner Renovo LLC, P.O. Box 966, Wake Forest, NC 27587.*

ISBN:978-0-9970275-0-1
1st Edition, January 2016

Table of Contents

Foreword

By Roby Mitchell, M.D. (Dr. Fitt)

Roby Mitchell, M.D. (Dr. Fitt)

We have an epidemic of epidemics. Despite the billions we spend on so called "healthcare," despite having the most medical doctors per capita of any country, despite being the world leader in medical technologies, despite having the best medical universities stocked with reams of medical journals, the United States has the worst medical, non-infectious disease outcomes of any nation on Earth. We have more heart disease, more cancer, more autoimmune disease, more Alzheimer's, more autism, more ADD/ADHD, more obesity, more food allergies, more high blood pressure, more osteoporosis, more high cholesterol, and more strokes than any other western culture. Americans spent $374 billion on prescription drugs in 2014, compared to Canada's $28 billion.

Any car manufacturer with the record of American medicine would have gone bankrupt years ago. How is it that American medicine manages to stay in business? The basics are the same as the recipe for a successful magic trick: the pledge, the presentation, and the prestige. The "pledge" is the portion of the trick where the magician explains the situation to you. He shows you an empty hat, an ordinary deck of cards or a woman in a box about to be sawed in half. In the doctor's office, the "pledge" is accomplished by an array of diagnostic equipment. It can be as simple as a blood pressure machine or as sophisticated as a PET scan or MRI. The "pledge" makes you aware of a situation. The "pledge" sets the stage for the rest of the deception.

The "presentation" is the critical part of any deception. The objective of the presentation is to distract you such that the third component, the "prestige," can be accomplished. The magician distracts you with a pretty assistant, hand gestures, playing on your preconceived ideas, or simply telling jokes. You're distracted just enough for the magician to accomplish the "prestige." In medicine, there is an elaborate "presentation." It starts with the doctor experience. The medical degree with your preconceived ideas about what that degree means, the nice office with pretty pictures, the sophisticated technology, the white coat all creates an experience akin to that first meeting with the Wizard of Oz. The "presentation" is complemented by television commercials that tell you to "see your doctor." If you buy the "presentation," the "prestige" is easy to accomplish. In magic, the "prestige" is sawing the woman in half then putting her back together. In medicine, the "prestige" is transferring your money to the doctors, hospitals and drug companies. It's an elaborate hoax.

I came to understand this through dealing with my own medical issues. By age 35, I had developed what is known in medicine as "metabolic syndrome." This consists of having high blood pressure, high blood sugar, high cholesterol, and a fat belly. This was despite the fact that I had been very physically active all my life and was a triathlete. My diet was not what it is now, but I ate better than most Americans.

> We have an epidemic of epidemics.

My push towards resolving these issues (that are risk factors for a heart attack) was when I had to treat a 37-year-old for that condition. Initially, I started a drug (beta blocker) to lower my blood pressure. This drug gave me so many side effects, it made me rethink things. My background was that in addition to doing the M.D. program at Texas Tech University School of Medicine, I was selected to be the first participant in a combined M.D/Ph.D. program.

My Ph.D. work was focused on high blood pressure and done under world-renowned physiologist and high blood pressure expert, Peter Pang, Ph.D., D. Sc. I harvested rat tails and put them in different solutions of magnesium, potassium, sodium and calcium. The upshot from these experiments was that magnesium and potassium lowered blood pressure and calcium and sodium raised blood pressure. When I revisited my Ph.D. notes and Guyton's Textbook of Medical Physiology, it hit me that what I needed to do was re-establish normal physiology, not adulterate it more with a drug.

Once I changed my diet to include more foods with potassium, replaced hydrochloric acid so that I would absorb magnesium, addressed my undiagnosed hypothyroidism and got rid of high salt foods, my blood pressure, cholesterol, and blood sugar returned to normal. So did my belly size. This fascinated me such that I began delving deeper into the healing power of foods. Medical science was saying most of the conditions we treat with drugs could be prevented, mitigated or reversed by simple diet changes. Why?

> *We impair the body's ability to heal itself when we interfere by using drugs that reduce fever.*

It turns out that most non-infectious western medical conditions are fueled by a condition called "inflammation." Cancer, asthma, Alzheimer's, osteoporosis, diabetes, autoimmune conditions, autism, acne, high blood pressure, strokes, high cholesterol, etc. are all driven by inflammation. Inflammation is the immune system's response to an elevated number of germs in your system. The fever, pain, redness, cough, nasal drainage, diarrhea, etc. are all caused not by the germs (critters) but by the immune system's response to an elevated number of critters. Even with Ebola, it's not the virus that kills you. It's your immune system's response to the virus.

The immune system has a vast array of "Weapons of Mass Destruction" termed "cytokines." The objective of cytokines is to bring critter levels back down to normal and repair any damage done by the process of inflammation. Prostaglandins, for instance, are cytokines that raise body temperature and cause fever. Critters don't like high temperatures. We impair the body's ability to heal itself when we interfere by using drugs that reduce fever. Leukotrienes, tumor necrosis factors, histamine, interleukins, growth factors, interferon, metalloproteinases, and macrophage stimulating factors are just a few of the cytokines produced by immune system cells.

Normally, the process of inflammation should last for a brief period. Critter levels should go back to normal and the symptoms from cytokines, like fever, should go away. The problem happens when inflammation becomes chronic. Long-term cytokine production destroys normal cells/tissues. The joint destruction seen with rheumatoid arthritis is a good example. The key to reversing western medical conditions is reducing inflammation. This means reducing critter counts.

Once I figured this out, I started looking at the impact of certain foods on critters. Plants live in an ambient environment of critters but don't have an immune system. They depend on bark, husks, peels, shells and an elaborate production of natural critter killers. I went to the lab and plated agar filled (critter food) petri dishes with Candida albicans. Candida is a common source of critter overgrowth in humans. Once Candida overgrows, it produces chemicals called "gliotoxins" that weaken the immune system. A weakened immune system will not be efficient in killing critters. This will make the inflammation process chronic. I added extracts from different foods to see which ones killed Candida the best. This was the genesis of the BALi Eating Plan®. When patients follow the BALi Eating Plan®, we see everything from acne to asthma and from diabetes to autoimmune conditions, reverse.

Simply BALi, A Complete Guide to a Healthy, Whole Foods Lifestyle, penned by Dawn Corridore and Jen Harris, takes the foods from my experiments and incorporates them into delicious recipes. Simply by eating great tasting food, you can prevent, reduce or reverse most western medical conditions not caused by infection, heavy metals or chemical ingestion. The book complements the eating plan with BALi lifestyle recommendations such as exercise, nutritional supplements, adequate rest and nourishing relationships. Follow this program for one month, *for the best of your life*.

> Simply by eating great tasting food, you can prevent, reduce or reverse most western medical conditions...

Introduction

Years ago, our ancestors ate the food that they were able to grow or catch themselves. The food grown in the soil was full of nutrients to nourish their bodies. There were no worries of genetically modified organisms (GMOs), pesticides, antibiotics in meat, preservatives and thousands of different chemicals in the food.

Today is a very different story. There are chemists whose sole job is to create a product that keeps you coming back for more, regardless of the health impacts. Many corporations add chemicals and preservatives to make the food last for years. The livestock is pumped full of hormones and antibiotics to make cows grow faster and larger.

You may feel alone changing your lifestyle and eating habits. You are NOT alone. As health coaches, we still have people coming to us wondering why macaroni and cheese is not healthy. Don't bury your head in the sand.

Take charge of the food you consume, the water you drink, and your body as a whole. Educate yourself to make the right decisions. This book was developed to help you do just that. We want to give you a starting point, a place to refer to when you are stuck on what to make for breakfast, lunch, dinner and snacks. We want you to also understand why these are healthy choices. This way you can use these recipes as a guide. If you do not have the ingredients on hand, feel free to change the recipes.

Here is a little more about us…

meet Dawn Corridore

I am a mom of two boys. Early on in their lives, my boys suffered with many "incurable" symptoms – allergies, irregular heartbeat, restrictive breathing at times, hives, eczema, mood swings, temper tantrums, tics and "ADD/ADHD."

After years of medicating, sleepless nights, crying to family and doctors (who turned a deaf ear), I felt like a failure. I knew something was not right. I knew with every fiber of my being that there had to be another way. So, I decided to start educating myself, looking for my own answers, and finding those experts who "heal" rather than "treat."

I started at my local health food store. This led me to a homeopath who guided my family and me to answers and placed us on the path of healing. DIET…it was about all diet. When the homeopath told me that "ALL" the symptoms that my children were experiencing were due to the foods I was feeding them every day, I immediately swallowed my pride, got my ego in check and made some very drastic changes in our diet and lifestyle.

After witnessing the "miracles" take place, not only in my children, but also with other members of my family and myself, I knew that I had to do something with this knowledge. This, I did. I went back to school to become a holistic health coach, I studied every book I could get my hands on and I learned from the experts who were getting real and permanent results. And while I still continue to educate myself, I now am able to educate, support and guide others to their path of healing.

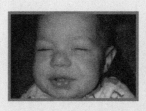

This is my son, Jason, at 12 months old. Though it may appear he had been crying, he had not. Here, his eyes are swollen shut, his face is swollen, he is congested and having difficulty breathing; this was Jason most days. For five years, I did everything the doctors told me to do until the day I said, "ENOUGH!" By educating myself, finding the right "healthcare" and implementing proper nutrition, Jason has been drug and symptom-free for 15 years and counting.

Two years ago I met and started studying under Roby Mitchell, M.D. It was at this time that my health really took off. He introduced me to the BALi Eating Plan®. He taught me to listen to my body and to go by symptoms, not just numbers from a lab report. I learned not to take advice from those who could not produce before and after photos. Since starting the BALi lifestyle, I feel as though my life has become clearer and more purposeful. I feel much better today at 48 than I did when I was 25.

What I love most about living a BALi lifestyle is I never have to worry about weighing anything or counting calories, carbs, proteins, or fats. I don't have to worry about what I ate for breakfast to know what I should eat for lunch or dinner, and I know from the transformation of my own health, that BALi will continue to keep critters under control and inflammation from wreaking havoc on my body.

GUIDING YOU TO
WELLNESS

Dawn can be reached at
www.GuidingYoutoWellness.com
Facebook: Guiding You to Wellness

meet Jen Harris

As a mother of two girls, I have had my share of ups and downs with both their health and my own. When my second daughter, Anna, was born, she was extremely sick. For the first year of her life, we were constantly in and out of doctors' offices and hospitals trying to get her healthy. At 9 months old, she became extremely lethargic and too weak to stand any more. She also could not keep anything down, including water. She was hospitalized, and the doctors were growing concerned that she might not make it. I finally said enough was enough. I forced our way into the offices of some of the top doctors in the Washington, D.C. area. Through many hours with them and hundreds of hours of research of my own, the doctors and I realized that the best way to heal her was through what she was ingesting.

I began to scrutinize every ingredient in the foods she was eating as well as the processing methods. After about three months of making healthy food choices for her, Anna began gaining weight. She continued her forward progress and as she got older even educated other children on healthy foods.

With everything I learned during the process to get her healthy, I thought about going back to school to help people learn the healing power of foods. Once her health was under control, though, I decided to go back and focus on my career as a Certified Public Accountant. I tried to eat healthy and exercise, but with my jam-packed schedule, it was really hard. I was often burning the candle at both ends trying to just keep up with life.

In May 2008, I was forced to stop everything. A car accident that left me with significant injuries to both my body and my mind forced me to retreat. I had to stop working and go through 3½ years of physical, vision, speech and cognitive therapies. To give you an idea of the impact… I couldn't remember how to take a shower, make a sandwich, get dressed, etc. Anytime I pushed my body or my mind beyond its capabilities at the time, I paid dearly for it. I learned to listen to signs and signals from my body. These signs were very important to my healing process.

During that healing process, I also developed a blistering, full body rash, which lasted for almost a year. It was NOT pretty. How did I get the rash to go away? After significant research and learning from some of the top minds in the field of nutrition, I again realized that food had the power to heal my body. I eliminated the items that did not serve my body well: processed foods, artificial sweeteners, chemical preservatives, food colorings and toxins in my household products. I began purchasing high quality foods, organic produce, grass-fed meats, and household products made with natural ingredients.

This was my wake-up call. I was not only able to heal my daughter through the healing power of food, but I was now able to heal myself as well. My life changed forever from that point on.

I went back to school to become a holistic health coach, so I could use this knowledge to help others.

The BALi Eating Plan® is actually very similar to the foods and lifestyle I had developed for myself. I have found that the foods on this plan really fuel my body best. They are the source of my energy. They support my constantly healing brain. They have helped to restore the health of my skin. The BALi foods and lifestyle are the fuel for my beautiful and amazing life.

...food had the power to heal my body

Shine for Life
Jen Harris, Holistic Health Coach

Jen can be reached at
www.ShineforLifeHHC.com
Facebook: Shine for Life HHC
Twitter: ShineforLifeHHC

Working Together...

Processed Foods

Inventions are seen as progress; however, the invention of processed foods has actually set back the health of many Americans. Years ago, people still valued real food. It was made from scratch. Ingredients were pronounceable.

Things began to change after the 1950s when the idea of shortcuts and faster foods became acceptable. Today, our processed foods resemble anything but their original ingredients. These processed foods often contain genetically modified ingredients, artificial colors, flavors and sweeteners. They're stabilized with chemical preservatives and then packaged in plastics that have been known to cause health problems.

These days, our lives are so busy that we consider fast food and eating out as convenient and reasonable time-savers over buying, preparing and cooking real food. The expiration date on the processed food at the grocery store, may be two years away. How is that possible? We know why, but oftentimes we ignore the preservatives and convince ourselves that it must be safe if they sell it.

The truth is simple…we need REAL food.

*The truth is simple…
we need REAL food.*

What is BALi?

The BALi Eating Plan® is not a short term, quick fix. It is a complete eating plan and lifestyle that is sustainable for the rest of your life.

As Roby Mitchell, M.D. (Dr. Fitt) was developing the BALi Eating Plan®, he went into the lab and tested foods to see which ones most effectively killed Candida albicans. According to Roby Mitchell, M.D., "When Candida overgrows, it produces gliotoxins. Gliotoxins are poison to your immune system cells. Once gliotoxins weaken your immune system, this allows overgrowth or infection by other critters (bacteria, viruses and fungi found in humans). The increased number of these critters is what leads to the immune system response of *Chronic Inflamation* that is the cause of most western medical conditions."

How is it Different From Paleo and Mediterranean Diets?

The difference between BALi, Paleo and the Mediterranean diets is the effectiveness of the food in helping you keep down your critter/yeast load and how much it raises blood sugar/insulin. Though Paleo and the Mediterranean diets have benefits, they do not offer the same principles to heal the body like BALi. BALi is focused primarily on low insulin production and the critter-killing potency of the products. BALi is effective because the foods have critter killing effectiveness (polyphenols, proanthocyanidins, allicin, resveratrol, etc.). The BALi Eating Plan® is the only eating plan designed specifically to bring down critter levels. Any eating plan that gets you off sugar and grains is a good start. However, consider what BALi stands for: Basic (Alkaline), Antioxidant/ Antifungal, Low insulin. BALi is about reducing the critter load by going after the reason(s) for critter overgrowth to begin with. BALi is an easy lifestyle to incorporate and sustain for a lifetime. We welcome you on the journey to become responsible for your own health.

What exactly does BALi mean?

B = Basic or alkaline. This refers to pH or acid balance. The lower the pH, the higher the acid content. BALi foods help your body maintain a slightly alkaline/basic pH of around 7.4. BALi fruits and veggies are alkaline.

A = Antioxidant/Antifungal. These are foods high in plant chemicals that kill fungus. These foods are distinguished by color, heat, and pungency. Plants make these chemicals to protect themselves from fungus. When you eat them, they protect you from fungal overgrowth. Usually, the darker the plant, the stronger its antioxidant/antifungal properties.

Li = Low insulin. These are foods that don't raise your blood sugar and insulin levels. If a food raises blood sugar, your body responds by producing more insulin. Insulin is the primary fat storage hormone.

Getting Started

The foods on the BALi Food List will make your blood more basic (or alkaline), control your body's level of Candida (a naturally occurring yeast), aid in insulin regulation, and increase your intake of antioxidants that can inhibit the ability of free radical damage.

The easiest way to begin making changes is to start with choices that are similar to your current foods. For instance, instead of white potatoes, choose purple or orange sweet potatoes. Choose grass-fed beef without added hormones instead of traditional beef. Choose eggs from free-range chickens.

To take these changes a step further, here are some more tips to get you started:

❖ Begin reading every label.

❖ Have a plan. Pick a day you can sit and plan out your meals. Also, make your shopping list. Then, pick another day to "shop and chop." You shop for all of your ingredients and you prep them as soon as you get home. To take it a step further, you can even pre-make your meals.

❖ Double your recipes. Prepare once, eat twice.

❖ Remove your triggers. If you are someone who would typically binge on a certain kind of snack food, then there is a good chance that you would binge on healthy versions of these as well.

❖ Move towards removing added sugars, anything "white" and unhealthy grains.

❖ Clean out your pantry. Life will become a whole lot easier as will achieving your goals to a more healthful lifestyle by taking this one step.

❖ If you feel "hungry" and you have eaten recently, consider drinking a glass of water and waiting 15 minutes. Oftentimes, you are simply dehydrated.

❖ Make healthy snacks and desserts for children to transition them off of the processed snacks with high fructose corn syrup, food colorings, genetically modified ingredients, etc. You can address the amount of sugars they consume after they have transitioned to these healthier versions.

❖ Know that your body is always craving and needing nutrients. Ask yourself these two questions before eating: "Is this going to provide my body with healthful nutrients? Is this food going to feed a toxic environment or support a healthy environment?"

❖ Aim for 5 to 9 cups of vegetables every day.

Keep in mind that sweet is sweet. Your brain does not know the difference between honey, stevia, or corn syrup. We know there are health benefits to some of these sweeteners (honey, stevia, xylitol, coconut sugar, blackstrap molasses) and that is why they are included on the list "in small amounts." The goal is to wean yourself off of the sweets to the point you are no longer craving them and/or daydreaming about them. We have to get used to less sweet foods. The more we eat the good stuff, the less we will crave the sweet stuff.

Sweeter = More Insulin
More Insulin = More Fat

A "sweet tooth" is the critters asking, craving, and demanding the sweet. Are you willing to feed them?

BALi Food List

(***** denotes antifungal/superfood)

BALi foods control your body's level of Candida (a naturally occurring yeast), aid in insulin regulation, and increase your intake of antioxidants that can inhibit free radical damage. Choose primarily fresh or frozen vegetables; organic, unpeeled fruits; low-mercury seafood; free-range poultry; grass-fed meat (without added hormones); raw nuts; beans and seeds; plant milks; organic, and raw cheese and yogurt.

Grilling/barbecuing is more likely to create chemicals that can potentially cause cancer. Marinating meat in rosemary, dark beer or red wine neutralizes this effect.

VEGETABLES & LEGUMES
Choose fresh or frozen
Acorn squash
Aduki beans
Arrowroot
Artichokes
Asparagus
Avocado
Beets
Black beans
Black radish
Bok choy
Broccoli
Brussels sprouts
*Cabbage (purple preferred)
Cactus
Carrots (purple preferred, unpeeled)
*Cauliflower (purple preferred)
Celery
*Chard (Swiss, rainbow)
Cherry tomatoes
Chives
*Cilantro
Collard greens
Cucumber
Eggplant
Endive
Fennel
Garbanzo beans
*Garlic
*Ginger
Green beans
*Green onion (scallions)
Kale (purple preferred)
Kidney beans
*Kohlrabi
*Leeks
Lentils
Lettuces (all but iceberg)
Lima beans
Mushrooms
Mustard greens
Okra

Olives
*Onions (red/purple)
Parsley
Parsnip
*Peppers (all types, hotter the better)
Pinto beans
Potatoes (purple, skin on)
Pumpkin
Radishes
Radicchio
Rhubarb
Rutabaga
Salad savoy
Shallots
*Soybeans/edamame (organic)
*Spinach
Sprouts (all types)
*Sprouts (Broccoli)
Sweet potatoes (regular or purple)
Squash (all)
Tofu
Tomatillo
Tomatoes
Turnips
Wasabi root
Yams
Yucca root
Zucchini

FRUITS & BERRIES
"Wild crafted" for best results – organic preferred – wash but don't peel – darker the better
*Acai (no added sugar)
Apples (Granny Smith, crab)
Avocados
*Blackberries
*Blueberries
Bitter melon
Boysenberries
Cherries (sour)
*Cranberries
*Coconut

*Currants (black, red)
*Elderberries
Figs
*Goji
Gooseberries
Grapefruit
Grapes (black)
Huckleberries
Key limes
Kiwi (fruit)
Kumquats
Lemons
Limes
Ligonberries
Mulberries
Oranges (blood)
Plums (black)
*Pomegranate
Prunes
Raspberries
Sea-buckthorn
Strawberries

NUTS
Raw, no salt
Almonds
Brazil nuts
Cashews
Chestnuts
Filberts
Hazelnuts
Macadamias
Pecans
Pine nuts
*Pistachios
Walnuts (black preferred)

SEEDS
Raw, no salt
Chia
*Cumin (black)
Flax
Hemp
Pumpkin
Sesame
Sunflower

FLOURS
Amaranth
Arrowroot
Artichoke
Barley
Buckwheat
Coconut
Einkorn

Kamut
Oat flour
Rye
Sorghum
Spelt
Teff

BEAN FLOURS
Black bean
Chickpea
Fava bean
Garbanzo bean
Kidney
Lentil

NUT FLOURS
Almond
Almond meal
Ground pecans
Ground walnuts

SEED FLOURS
Flaxseed (ground)
Hemp seed
Pumpkin seed flour/meal
Quinoa
Sesame seed meal
Sunflower seed meal

Baking powder (aluminum-free)
Baking soda

GRAINS & PASTA
Amaranth
Artichoke pasta
Barley
Black bean pasta
Brown rice noodles
Buckwheat
Kamut
Mung bean pasta
Non-yeasted breads
Oats-Irish/steel cut (preferred)
Oats (rolled, not instant)
Oat bran
Oatmeal
Quinoa-black, red
Quinoa pasta
Rice-black, red
Rye
Soba
Soba noodles
*Sorghum
Spelt
Spinach pasta

Sprouted grain breads/pasta
Teff

BUTTERS & OILS
Organic, raw
BUTTERS
Almond butter
Butter
Coconut butter
Ghee

OILS
Avocado
Almond
*Black seed
*Coconut
*Extra Virgin Olive Oil (EVOO)
*Fish oil
Flax
Grapeseed
*Pistachio nut
Sesame
Sunflower
Walnut

DAIRY
Organic, raw
Butter
Coconut yogurt
Ghee
Goat cheese/milk/yogurt
Kefir
Milk (raw)
Raw milk
Sour cream
Yogurt (plain)

CHEESES
Organic, raw, w/out rBGH
& antibiotics

Asiago
Blue cheese
Cheddar
Cottage cheese
Cream cheese
Feta
Goat
Mozzarella
Parmesan
Ricotta

ALTERNATIVE MILK
Almond milk (unsweetened)
Coconut milk (unsweetened)

Goat milk (unsweetened)
Hemp milk (unsweetened)

FISH / SHELLFISH
Smaller fish = less mercury
Anchovies
Cod
Crab
Halibut
Orange roughy
*Salmon (wild caught)
*Sardines
Shrimp
Trout
*Tuna
Other fish (canned, fresh)

POULTRY
Chicken (free range)
Duck (Cornish hens & others)
Eggs
Goose
Pheasant
Turkey

RED MEATS
Grass-fed, antibiotic free
Antelope
Beef
Bison
Bonsmara beef
Buffalo
Lamb
Ostrich
Pork (uncured, unsmoked)
Rabbit
Squirrel
Veal
Venison
Wild game

SAUCES/CONDIMENTS
Bragg Liquid Aminos
Bragg Herbs & Spices
Capers
Cardamon
*Cayenne pepper
Chilies
Chili powder
Chili sauce

Chinese mustard
Chipotle
*Cinnamon
Coriander
*Cumin (ground)
*Cumin (black seed)
*Curry powder
Dijon mustard
Fennel
*Garlic (fresh)
Garlic powder
Ginger
Gomasio (sea salt & seaweed)
Honey (raw, unrefined, organic)
*Kelp
Ketchup (organic, sugar-free)
*Kim chee
Lemon juice
Lime juice
Marinara sauce (sugar-free)
Miso
Mustard
Nigella (onion seed)
Nutmeg
Nutritional yeast
Olives
Onion powder
*Oregano
Pesto
Pickles
Red chili paste
*Rosemary
Sage
Salsa
*Sauerkraut
Sea salt
Sesame seed
Sriracha
Tamari
Tarragon
Tabasco
Tomato paste
*Turmeric
Vanilla
Vegenaise mayonnaise
Vinegar

SWEETENERS
Cacao
Cinnamon

Coconut palm sugar
Honey (raw, unrefined, organic)
Luo Han Guo (Lo Han)
Maple syrup (pure)
Molasses (blackstrap, organic)
Nutmeg
Stevia
Vanilla
*Xylitol
Yacon

BEVERAGES
Water
Coconut water
Water (purified/filtered)
Water (sparkling)

JUICE
Juice made from small,
dark, bitter fruits. Smoothies and
juices (more veggies than fruit).
Organic preferred.
Currant
Pomegranate
Purple carrot
Tart cherry

COFFEE (*organic)
The darker the roast, the more
processed
Light roast (preferred)

TEAS (*organic)
Black
Green
Herbal teas
Kombucha
Pau D'Arco
*White (preferred)

WEAPONS OF
MASS REDUCTION
B Complex 75
Black seed oil
*Eco Thyro (Recommend an evaluation
before taking)
IodoRX
Magnesium gel
Selenium
Vitamin D3

minerals and antioxidants than whole grains. Phytic acid is destroyed when the grain sprouts, so your body is able to absorb the nutrients in these grains - which makes them that much better for you!

Our favorite sprouted grain bread is the Ezekiel 4:9 Sprouted Grain Bread by Food for Life. It's made from six different organic sprouted grains and absolutely no flour! This combo of sprouted grains contains all nine essential amino acids, which makes up a complete protein. There are no preservatives in these breads, so you need to keep them in your freezer and take out portions as you need them. They are available in most health food stores and some conventional stores in the freezer section.

Other breads can be purchased. Choose breads made from grains and flours on the BALi Food List. Ideally, these breads would have five ingredients or less.

Similar to wheat breads, gluten-free bread often contains lots of added ingredients, including sugar, agave nectar and evaporated cane juice. If you must avoid gluten due to an allergy, it's best to choose seed-based breads or BALi-friendly tortillas.

Sprouted grain bread contains more vitamins, minerals and antioxidants than whole grains.

BALi-Approved
Flours and Their Uses

When it comes to flour, there's no longer a one-size-fits-all approach. There are many different flours available to create delicious recipes. Experimenting with different types of flours can boost the nutritional variety in your diet. For instance, nut flours can increase both the moisture and the protein content of a recipe, but you do need to use the information below when substituting other flours for regular all-purpose flour to ensure your recipe is successful.

Tips On Using Alternative Flours

❖ The weight of your flour is crucial. One cup of all-purpose flour weighs 125 grams so you would want to substitute the all-purpose flour with 125 grams of alternative flour. Depending on what alternative flour you use, you may use less or more than one cup.

❖ Flours higher in proteins work best for crusts, biscuits, rolls, and breads. Flours with lower proteins work best for cakes, brownies, and cookies.

❖ It is best to store flours in airtight containers and in dark cool places.

❖ Protein and starch: Protein is important because it provides the structure to your baked goods. The starch, on the other hand, provides the tenderness. Both are important when baking gluten-free. For a nice balance, you'd typically want 70% protein flour and 30% starch flour.

❖ Try to use more than one alternative flour. It has been documented that by combining different flours you will achieve better results.

See the chart on the next page for explanations of each flour type and how it can be used.

Flours

AMARANTH FLOUR (120G)
Amaranth flour is very high in protein, which makes for nutritious baking.

ARROWROOT FLOUR (130G)
Arrowroot flour is typically used for thickening recipes and can be used in place of cornstarch and tapioca.

BARLEY FLOUR (115G)
Barley flour has very little gluten. It has a bit of a nutty flavor. This flour can be used to thicken recipes but if combined with another alternative flour, it can be used for cakes, biscuits and pastries.

BEAN FLOURS (range from 120G to 150G)
This would include your black bean, chickpea, garbanzo bean, and lentil. These flours are high in protein and best suited for breads and other substantial recipes.

BUCKWHEAT FLOUR (120G)
Just to be clear, buckwheat is not a form of "wheat." Buckwheat flour has more of a nutty flavor. If used alone it could take on a bitter and overpowering taste.

CHIA FLOUR (163G)
Chia flour can easily be made by grinding the seeds in a coffee grinder. If using chia flour for baking, you will want to slightly increase your liquids and baking time.

COCONUT FLOUR (115G)
When substituting with coconut flour, you will want to increase the liquid amount. Coconut flour can be used alone. This flour is low in carbohydrates and very high in fiber.

NUT FLOURS (range from 110G to 115G)
Any nut will do. Pick your nut of choice and grind it into a powder. Nut flours are very high in protein so they would not convert equally for other flours. They are best used mixed with other flours.

OAT FLOUR (120G)
Oat flour can easily be made by grinding the oats in a coffee grinder. Oat flour will require more liquid since it absorbs liquids more than other flours. Oat flour is a good alternative to make cookie and cake recipes. If a recipe calls for yeast, you will want to use more with oat flour than you would with all-purpose flour. Typically you would use $1\frac{1}{2}$ cups oat flour in place of one cup of wheat flour.

QUINOA FLOUR (110G)
This flour adds a nutty flavor to baked goods. It is best used for scones, biscuits and pancakes.

RYE FLOUR (light 100G, dark 120G)
Rye flour is good for making breads, pancakes and muffins. Rye flour is denser than other alternative flours. This flour does contain gluten.

SORGHUM FLOUR (135G)
Sorghum flour is great to use for making flat unleavened breads and porridge.

SPELT FLOUR (100G)
Spelt flour is very similar to wheat in baking. Spelt flour contains gluten and because it does, it is a good choice for baking bread. Spelt has more protein and fiber than wheat.

TEFF FLOUR (100G)
Teff flour has a nutty flavor and is loaded with nutrients. Teff is a great flour to use in combination with other flours.

Setting Up Your Kitchen

A typical grocery store is filled with processed, packaged items that barely resemble real food. This guide will help set you up for success with healthy eating. A well-organized pantry is a secret weapon to save time, money and stress in the kitchen. Just follow these steps to get organized today!

The Cleanout

You may have done this with your closets before. This phase requires you to take everything — yes, EVERYTHING — out of your pantry. If we just look through our pantry, we often overlook items we should toss. By physically taking an item out, it will then have to go through several steps before it makes it back into your pantry. Once you have taken everything out, wipe it down, vacuum it…do whatever you need to do to clean it up.

Should I Toss It?

You want to rid your environment of all non-BALi foods. In this step, you will go through each and every item for the following criteria:

❖ Has it expired? If yes, toss it.

❖ Is it filled with ingredients not suitable for your family (dyes, preservatives, chemicals, etc.) or not on the BALi Food List? If yes, consider donating it to a local food pantry or tossing it.

❖ Is it regular pasta? If so, donate or toss it, replacing it with a BALi-approved pasta.

❖ Is it white or brown rice? If so, donate or toss it, replacing it with red and/or black rice.

How to Organize It

Oftentimes it is easiest to organize by taking foods out of boxes/packages. The packaging can be so bulky that it just takes up too much room.

❖ Canned items – store them together, but in categories (beans together, soups together, etc.).

❖ Pasta and rice – store these in the same area.

❖ Baking items – store these items together.

❖ Snacks and granola bars – store these items together.

Dining Out Tips

Eating out should not cause you to panic.
Use these tips to help make the best choices.

❖ Choose restaurants that serve local, organic foods, if possible.

❖ Go places where you can eat with a fork.

❖ Research the restaurant before going. Many put their menus online; plan your meal prior to arriving. If the menu is not online, call to see what they offer. Making a decision before can keep you from being tempted by the sight of other choices.

❖ Modify the menu. Foods are often batter-dipped and fried, so make special requests. Many restaurants will take your dietary needs into account so you'll be a happy customer and return. Don't hesitate to request anything on the menu to be prepared a different way.

Good Choices:

❖ Steak, chicken, Alaskan salmon and shrimp

❖ Steamed vegetables

❖ Black or kidney beans with no rice

❖ Salads with LOTS of vegetables – look over their entrée salad choices; choose spinach or mixed greens, then ask them to add all of the vegetables you see from any of the salads listed on the menu. If they are on the menu, then they should have them!

❖ Choose dressings carefully – ask for oil and vinegar to top your salad.

❖ Bring your own salad protein topper (if there is no good alternative) such as sliced almonds, walnuts, ground flax seeds or hemp seeds. When your salad arrives, add your own protein.

❖ Order water with lemon as a drink (squeeze the lemon in your water, then put it to the side – don't just drop it in due to the chemicals on the lemon rind).

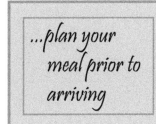

...plan your meal prior to arriving

Time Savers

Let's face it. Our lives are often very full. You CAN find the time to eat healthy. Here are a few tips to show you how.

General

❖ *Get organized* – There's no better way to save time in the kitchen than to have easy access to all of your tools and ingredients. One good organizational strategy is to put like items together. Plot out the storage space in your kitchen and inventory all the stuff you need to find a home for. Keep sections for the most frequently used items close to the central work areas like the stove, sink and refrigerator. If you have peripheral storage, as in a kitchen island or breakfast room, reserve it for items you use less frequently.

❖ *Keep the basics on hand* – To make life easier at mealtime, keep the basics on hand in your cupboards. Staples like herbs, spices, grains and oils store well. Ground flaxseed, chia seeds, and nuts should be stored in the refrigerator or the freezer. If you know that you use onions, purple carrots, celery, fresh garlic or sweet potatoes often in cooking, stock up. If you have a regular inventory and rotate it efficiently, you'll be able to save time and the stress of last minute shopping. You'll also be able to plan your buying efforts better.

❖ *Clean off your counters* – Over time, you lose precious counter space in the kitchen. Appliance creep starts innocently enough with the addition of a toaster and then slowly grows to include the food processor, mini mixer, can opener, toaster oven, and on and on. Store these items somewhere else (cabinets, a pantry, nearby closet). Unless you use the appliance every day, it should not be on your counters. This will make your work in the kitchen more efficient by eliminating excess clutter.

❖ *Cook in batches* – If you want to save money as well as time in the kitchen, try consolidating your efforts by cooking large batches of food and freezing what you don't use right away. Consider making a bunch of your meals for the week on the weekend. One afternoon or evening is all you need to make enough food for a week's worth of meals or more. After that, just defrost and reheat.

❖ *Use a crock-pot* – All you have to do is add the ingredients, close the lid and turn the crock-pot on. You can literally prepare a one-pot meal with 10 minutes worth of effort. The great part is that it'll taste like you worked on it all day. These are perfect for those who get home late and need to get food on the table quickly. Crock-pots save you time with cleanup, too. There's just one pot to clean and the plates, of course.

❖ *While dinner is cooking*, make tomorrow's lunch.

❖ *Clean as you go* – Keep the sink full of warm, soapy water to clean measuring cups, pots, and utensils as you go. Then, after dinner, you will simply have plates, serving bowls and utensils to put in the dishwasher.

❖ *Get your kids to help*! They need to learn how to juggle activities, homework and helping around the house. Obviously, this needs to be age appropriate.

❖ *Maximize shelf life* and minimize waste for raw and cooked foods. The website stilltasty.com will tell you just how long things can stay in your refrigerator, pantry or freezer.

Food Preparation

❖ Prepare vegetables in advance. Cut up enough veggies to last a few days, both for snacking and cooking. For those that need even faster preparation, pick up pre-cut vegetables in the produce section at your local grocery store or health food store.

❖ Quick and easy way to take the stems off the kale – just hold the kale upside down by the stems and pull the leaves off by just sliding your hand along the stem. Kids love helping with this.

❖ Use organic frozen vegetables and fruit to save time, if possible.

❖ If using canned beans, make sure you rinse them very well. Look for BPA-free cans. Some canned beans also include kombu. Kombu is edible kelp that makes the beans more digestible. These beans are available at your local health food store or online.

❖ Double the smoothie recipe in the morning and have it as a snack. If the smoothie feels too cold in your body, blend it several more times. This will help to warm it up. You can also add more warming spices to it (cinnamon, cloves, nutmeg, cayenne, turmeric, cardamom, and/or ginger).

❖ Use canned or frozen wild Alaskan salmon.

How to Store Fresh Herbs (parsley, cilantro and other fresh herbs)

Snip off the bottom of the stems. Make sure the leaves are completely dry. Hold off rinsing them until you're about to use them. Fill a jar or a water glass partially with water and place the stem ends of the herbs into the water in the jar. If you are storing the herbs in the refrigerator, cover loosely with a plastic bag. Cilantro loves cool temperatures and should be stored in the refrigerator. Parsley can be stored at room temperature or in the refrigerator. Basil is ideally stored at room temperature and not in the refrigerator, because it is susceptible to damage from cold. Change the water after several days if

the water starts to discolor. Fresh parsley, cilantro, basil, and other fresh herbs can last up to two weeks or longer when stored this way.

Cooking Tips and Techniques

❖ Cook chicken in advance for some of the recipes and salads. Poached chicken breasts are easy to make in advance; they retain their moisture, and you can use them in all kinds of recipes for salads, wraps and soups.

❖ If you do not have time to chop vegetables, use the shredding blade on your food processor. If you do not have a food processor, check Amazon for reasonably-priced ones (as low as $30).

❖ Spice up your food. Add herbs and spices to your cooking. Adding fresh rosemary, chopped cilantro, chives, or parsley helps enhance the flavor and reduces the need to add fat. You can also add fresh crushed garlic to your vegetables.

❖ Expand your horizons; you're sure to find something new and tasty to enhance your meals. Try eating vegetables from all categories.

more economical way to enjoy your fish.

Plain Organic or Greek Yogurt

Yogurt contains live and active cultures of "good" bacteria, which promotes a healthy gut. Yogurt is a great source of protein and can be eaten alone, in smoothies and can replace sour cream. To be more cost effective, consider buying the large container instead of the small individual cups.

Organic Eggs

Eggs are a low-cost, high-quality protein source. One egg contains 6 grams of protein. They are a quick and healthful choice anytime of the day. Eggs are very useful in a variety of dishes. Consider purchasing the large carton of eggs (18 or more) and from a local farmer.

Sweet Potatoes

An excellent source of beta carotene which your body will convert to vitamin A if thyroid levels are adequate, they are also loaded with vitamin C and B vitamins. Sweet potatoes are a great

antioxidant food and pack a healthy fiber punch! Sweet potatoes can be enjoyed for breakfast, lunch, and dinner or for a snack.

Almonds

Nuts may have a reputation for being pricey, but they are actually very budget-friendly, especially when you consider that one ounce is a proper portion for a snack (that's about 22 almonds). Almonds are a great source of heart-healthy unsaturated fat, vitamin E and protein. So enjoy them — just do so in moderation.

Quinoa

Full of calcium, iron and B vitamins, quinoa is also high in protein. The fluffy texture makes it a fun alternative to rice and it cooks up quicker than rice.

Black Rice

There is not enough said about the benefits from black rice. It's high in protein, iron, fiber and also an excellent antioxidant food. If bought it bulk, you can really save your pennies.

Redefine Breakfast, Lunch & Dinner

Traditionally, many of us have been taught to eat cereal, oatmeal, eggs, sausage, bacon, toast, muffins, and pancakes for breakfast. Lunch for most Americans consists of sandwiches. Then, dinner is considered to be a hearty meal. Humans are the only species that have assigned specific foods to specific meals at specific times in the day.

We need to re-think these habits.

Let's start with the first meal of the day. As the word implies, breakfast literally means, "breaking the fast" since it's the first meal you eat after you wake. After this "fast," it's time to nurture your hungry brain and body with delicious, healthful foods. This doesn't have to mean eggs, pancakes, or cereal. Any food that can fuel your body for the day ahead will suffice. In fact, consider filling the crock-pot the night before with a meal, so you can enjoy it for breakfast one day, lunch the next and dinner the following day.

Breakfast for dinner is accepted; however, the concept of having dinner for breakfast makes many uncomfortable.

Redefining breakfast, lunch and dinner is not as much about eating burgers for breakfast and eggs for dinner as it is about freeing you from the constraints of traditional breakfast, lunch and dinner foods. Go ahead and eat beef stew, butternut squash, sweet potatoes, chicken soup, chicken salad, and green salads for breakfast! Enjoy omelets, pancakes and smoothies for lunch and dinner!

Stop putting restrictions on your meals.
Enjoy your leftovers at breakfast.
Reprogram, explore and start
enjoying all of your meals.

How to Stay on
Track for the Holidays

The holidays are a time to gather around with friends and family and celebrate. For many though, it's the time of year when they give themselves permission to enjoy all of the unhealthy foods that go along with the holidays.

How do you enjoy the holidays without paying for it months and years down the road? Do you need to keep yourself locked inside, away from all of the parties, pies, cookies, mixed drinks, etc.? Of course not! It may take some planning and even some discipline, but you can enjoy the holidays along with everyone else. Here are just a few tips to keep you on track for all of your holiday festivities.

Hydrate

Begin your day with a large glass of water and make sure to drink water throughout the day. The best way to stay hydrated is to drink hot water with sea salt throughout the day. Plain hot water is fine too. Just be sure to DRINK! Number one reason we feel hungry... DEHYDRATION!

Exercise in the Morning

Be sure to exercise every morning during the holidays. This is very important! Get up 30 minutes earlier if necessary. When we exercise, we feel better about ourselves and when we feel better about ourselves, it's easier to make healthier food choices.

Keep a Food Journal

We are big fans of journaling, especially if you are a newbie. Journaling is essential on holidays. One...It makes you accountable. Two...It makes you pause and give thought to what you are about to eat. Three...It will remind you what you had three hours prior that you forgot you had. Be honest with yourself. You will not be cheating anyone but yourself if you are not.

Begin With a Healthy Breakfast

Have a big, healthy breakfast that includes a BIG green smoothie. Make extra so you can have another before your big meal.

Prepare

If you know there will be no good food choices, then you MUST prepare and bring your own food. Bring your entire meal if necessary and do not feel bad about it. Remember why you started this journey. Be sure this meal includes a dessert and/or snack, especially if you are a snacker or cannot bear to see someone else eating things you once loved. Another option is to eat before you go. Then, you can simply have a salad or soup and whatever dessert/snack you made for yourself.

Avoid Alcohol

Try to avoid alcohol. We have found with our clients that when they consume alcohol, they are less in control to make healthful choices.

Exercise After You Eat

Weather permitting, persuade everyone to go on a nice leisurely walk after your largest meal. If the weather is not cooperating, suggest games like Charades, Twister, or Wii games (bowling, golf, baseball, etc.). Choose games that will get you moving. Another idea is to simply turn on the music and dance.

Tea Before Dessert

Thirty minutes before dessert, make yourself a cup of hot dandelion tea with one tablespoon of coconut oil. You did bring a BALi-friendly dessert, right?

Brush Your Teeth

When you are done with dessert, excuse yourself to go brush your teeth. Then, chew a couple pieces of xylitol gum. This will signal your body and mind that you are done eating. It will also keep your mouth busy, so you will not go after leftovers.

No Excuses

Do not give yourself or allow someone else to give you permission to eat something that is going to feed sickness. You know what we are talking about...."Just this one day." "One piece is not going to hurt me?" "It's Thanksgiving." "I'm too thin anyway." "I can afford a piece." "I'll get right back to it tomorrow." "I'll work out extra hard tomorrow." DON'T DO IT. A little poison is not okay, EVER!

BALi Testimonial

"I was 48 years old when I decided I was going to change my life. I wanted to be healthy, so when I'm at the ripe age of 65+, I wouldn't be dependent on prescription drugs. My mother is very unhealthy, and I knew I did not want to end up like her, sick and dependent. This was the path I was on though.

I started with the Atkins Diet, which is very limited on what you can eat. I did that for a couple of years with very little change in my health and body. When Dawn Corridore started educating me on the importance of eating the right foods for my body and introducing me to the BALi Eating Plan®, things began to happen. I started implementing the knowledge and tools that had been given to me, and found by eating healthier, the weight goes away and your body starts healing and feeling better.

Presently, I am eating BALi and cooking at home seven days a week; my husband and I have been together for 13 years and we dined out almost every day. I never thought I would find myself saying this, but I totally enjoy cooking at home and knowing that the foods I'm eating are not only very good for me, but they are very satisfying.

When I started, I was right at 200 pounds and a size 14/16. It was very depressing and I was not feeling comfortable in my clothes. I have been doing the BALi Eating Plan® for a year and a half now. I am 150 pounds and a size 4/6. I feel happy when I look in the mirror and see a healthier person. I have much more energy and my mood has improved immensely. I love getting dressed and feeling comfortable in my clothes. I have adjusted to eating healthier and the junk food that I once craved, I no longer desire."

Angie McCoon
Fresno, CA

Going Beyond Food

The BALi Lifestyle

In order to be healthy, we must be in balance. This includes diet, exercise, sleep, stress management, relationships, self-care, healthy elimination, sex and gratitude. Together these fuel the energy in our lives. If any one of these areas is out of balance, we often search for other ways to satisfy those needs. Many people use comfort foods. Think back to a time in your life when you were facing a major life change. How did you cope? Think about where you stand in each of these areas. You can also use the reference pages in the back of the book to journal your thoughts and feelings on each area.

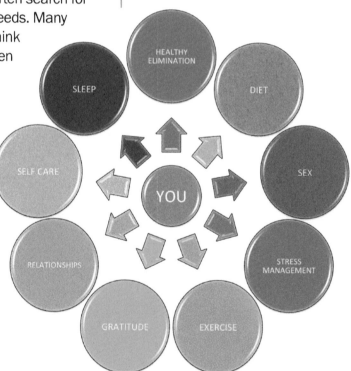

Diet

Diet is responsible for 85% of our overall health and well-being. The proper diet provides us with the right nutrients, without excess or deficiency, to maintain great health. With a healthful diet, we can reach and maintain a healthy weight, reduce our risk of high blood pressure, high cholesterol, diabetes, obesity, autoimmune disease, inflammation, and even cancer. Our body thrives on the proper nutrients to feed our organs, tissues and cells. The BALi Eating Plan® takes the guesswork out and provides us with everything our body needs to thrive.

Exercise

"To enjoy the glow of good health, you must exercise."
– Gene Tunney

Exercise improves our overall health and well-being. Exercise aids our body in transporting oxygen and nutrients throughout our body; oxygen and nutrients are needed to fuel the cells that fight bad bacteria and viruses. Physical activity will give us all the energy we need. Exercise improves our cardiovascular system; an improved cardiovascular system can then get the oxygen and nutrients to our muscles. Mood is another thing that improves when we incorporate exercise. Exercise stimulates the release of endorphins, which make us feel happier and more relaxed. Physical actively reduces stress. When stress is reduced, we can better cope with life's challenges and avoid depression. When choosing exercises, be certain to pick the things that you will enjoy and activities that are sustainable for a lifetime.

There are many things to choose from:

❖ Join a gym

❖ Join a local boot camp

❖ Purchase and use exercise DVDs

❖ Practice yoga

❖ Join a Pilates class

> *"Let food be thy medicine and medicine be thy food."*
> *Hippocrates*

❖ Swim

❖ Dance

❖ Nordic pole walk

❖ Hike

❖ Participate in sports

❖ Run

❖ Use a BOSU (Both Sides Utilized) Balance Trainer

❖ Rebound (jumping on a mini trampoline)

❖ Lift weights or body resistance

Sleep

Sleep is the time our bodies rest, rejuvenate, heal and replace old cells with new ones. When we do not provide our bodies with the proper amount of sleep, then they cannot perform the necessary functions. Being sleep deprived can contribute to weight-gain, hormone imbalances, brain fog, diabetes, cardiovascular disease, depression and even cancer. By getting at least seven hours of sleep per night, we can minimize the

risk of these things happening. We will also likely feel more energetic, vibrant and happier.

Tips for a more restful sleep:

❖ Eat a clean and balanced diet

❖ Hydrate throughout the day

❖ Avoid eating three hours before bed

❖ Use one teaspoon of magnesium gel rubbed into the skin nightly

❖ Turn off all stimulants two hours before bedtime (TV, computers, smartphones)

❖ Avoid caffeine

❖ Darken your room (the darker the better)

❖ Keep the temperature in your room cooler

❖ Do not eat sugars or grains after lunchtime

❖ Journal before bed. Write down all the stressors that occurred throughout your day…leave them on the paper

❖ Meditate for 15 minutes

❖ Practice deep breathing

Sleep is that golden chain that ties health and our bodies together."

Thomas Dekker

❖ Place pure, essential lavender oil behind your ears

❖ Diffuse lavender or other essential oils in your bedroom

Stress Management

"The greatest weapon against stress is our ability to choose one thought over another."
– William James

Stress hormones, cortisol and adrenaline are all being released every time we stress, not to mention blood vessels constrict, heart rate increases, breathing becomes more rapid, and blood pressure goes up. This is not a good thing. When these things take place, stress can easily become chronic, which can impact your overall health. Let's take a look at how stress can affect our health. Stress can cause hormone imbalances, affect our sleep, cause our body to store fat, raise blood pressure and raise blood sugar. It can cause digestive issues, hair loss, aging, can lead to depression, cardiovascular disease, etc. In a nutshell, stress will wreak havoc on our mental and physical well-being.

Tips to alleviate stress:

❖ Eat a healthful and balanced diet

❖ Exercise

❖ Meditate/breathe

❖ Use essential oils to help you relax

❖ Remove grains and sugars

❖ Get more sleep

❖ Serve others

❖ Find things that make you laugh

❖ Walk/hike in nature

❖ Drink chamomile tea and/or herbal teas

❖ Remove caffeine

❖ Remove alcohol

❖ Be present

❖ Let go of things you have no control over

❖ Journal

❖ Spend time with happy people

Relationships

Healthy relationships are vital for good health, mentally, physically and spiritually. Healthy relationships contribute to experiencing a happy, joyful and more

fulfilling life. Many of our stressors come from our interactions with other people, especially those with whom we have encounters on a daily basis (family, neighbors, co-workers, etc.). We all thrive best when we have nurturing relationships. It is so important that we enjoy the people we spend time with. We believe most of us have a person or two that we have no choice but to spend time with. We have all experienced negative emotions and buttons being pushed by others. However, it is through our relationships that we learn a great deal about ourselves, evolve and grow. Relationships should rank pretty high on our priority list. Any health regimen that does not include ways to improve relationships is incomplete.

Tips on improving relationships:

❖ Improving relationships starts as an inside job

❖ Become who you truly want to be

❖ Treat others the way you'd want to be treated

❖ Take responsibility for your own actions and outcomes

❖ Stop trying to control others and situations

❖ Let go of unhealthy and/or abusive relationships

❖ Create a safe environment for others to approach you

❖ Figure out why certain people cause you to react negatively

❖ Stop pointing fingers and placing blame

❖ Learn to resolve conflicts

❖ Respect others' opinions even when they differ from yours

❖ Communicate clearly and openly

❖ Be honest

❖ Let go of expectations

❖ Be kind

❖ Learn to walk away and breathe before responding and/or reacting

❖ Express love and give love daily

> *"Intense love does not measure, it just gives."*
> Mother Teresa

❖ Love is unconditional, remove conditions

Self-Care

Nurturing one's self is often non-existent for most, yet it is crucial in maintaining a healthy body, mind, relationships and lifestyle. We must put the oxygen mask on ourselves first. If we are sick, exhausted, depressed, undernourished, and barely coping, then what service are we truly going to be to others? We can only pretend for so long before our health declines to the point of no return. A lot of people associate self-care with selfishness, unworthiness or even being lazy. This is programming at its finest. This must be revisited. When we are well nurtured we can better serve others, our relationships improve, we are happier and feel more willing to take on new things, our senses are heightened, and we are able to live on purpose. Self-care is a very individual thing so though we are providing a tips list here, please do the things that best serve you.

Tips for self-care:

❖ Get out in nature

❖ Walk the beach

❖ List the things that you love about yourself

❖ Soak in a hot Epsom salt and lavender bath

❖ Go for a massage

❖ Do yoga

❖ Perform acts of kindness

❖ Be mindful

❖ Go dancing

❖ Eat healthy foods

❖ Read that book you have been putting off

❖ Have sex with your partner

❖ De-clutter

❖ Meditate

❖ Buy something new

❖ Make pottery

❖ Go horseback riding

❖ Take a day to rest

❖ Learn something new

❖ Let go of the things that do not serve you

❖ Be playful

" The greatest tool for self-love is self-awareness. Once you truly know yourself, love is the only option. "
Vironika Tugaleva

Healthy Elimination

Constipation is a huge contributor to poor health. If our body does not rid the toxic waste daily then those toxins can be absorbed back into the body. The longer we go without a bowel movement, the weaker our immune system becomes and the more toxic our bodies become. We can experience fatigue, irritability, headaches, bloating, gas, bad breath, weight gain, hemorrhoids, and colon cancer. Furthermore, our body's ability to absorb nutrients becomes compromised. Since bowel movements affect our entire physiology, we should not ignore them. If we are making good food and lifestyle choices then we should be producing comfortable and healthy bowel movements. If we are eliminating daily, than we can have peace of mind knowing our colons are in good health.

> *"People can tell a measure of their health by their bowel movements."*
>
> Ted Loftness, M.D.

Tips to have healthy bowel movements:

❖ Incorporate a healthful and balanced diet

❖ Remove processed food

❖ Remove bad grains and sugars

❖ Hydrate

❖ Get plenty of fiber

❖ Get plenty of healthful fats

❖ Exercise

❖ De-stress

❖ Massage one teaspoon of magnesium gel onto your body daily

❖ Be sure you are getting enough Vitamin D3

❖ Be sure your stomach is producing enough hydrochloric acid

❖ Eliminate when you feel the urge, do not wait

❖ Consume fermented food

❖ Squat like a toddler when eliminating

❖ Check that TSH is below 1 (as per Roby Mitchell, M.D.)

❖ Hypothyroidism can cause constipation

Sex

Sex is a part of nature.
I go along with nature."
– Marilyn Monroe

Yes, we have to go there. Many of us are living sexless lives and we are here to tell you that you are leaving out a very important component to having an overall, well-balanced and healthy life. The benefits from having sex are endless. It helps with sleep because after an orgasm, the body releases hormones like prolactin and oxytocin, all associated with sleep. Sex may lower stress levels, burn calories, strengthen the immune system, improve the skin, boost self-esteem, lower blood pressure, strengthen the heart, reduce pain in the body due to endorphins being released during orgasm, and some studies have suggested that orgasms can lower the risk of prostate cancer in men and breast cancer in women. Sex is a very individual thing. Though we are providing a tip list, go by what feels right to you.

Tips on improving your sex life:

❖ Eat a healthful diet

❖ Consume aphrodisiac foods (oysters, avocados, figs, dark chocolate, olives, dark cherries, pumpkin seeds, purple-colored foods, maca, and even chili peppers)

❖ Create a safe environment

❖ Communicate openly and honestly

❖ Self explore – know what brings you pleasure and what does not so you can communicate this

❖ Take time to simply touch

❖ Relax

❖ Be playful

❖ Be spontaneous

❖ Put sex on the calendar

❖ Compliment your partner

❖ Be respectful

"Acknowledging the good you already have in your life is the foundation for all abundance."
Eckhart Tolle

Gratitude

Giving thanks daily could have tremendous benefits on our mind, health and our lives. We all have the ability to recognize things in our lives to be grateful for. It's as simple as taking a few minutes a day to focus on all the things that we have instead of focusing on the things we do not have. Gratitude can help us put things in perspective and help us see clearer. Gratitude is not something we are typically taught but it is something worth acquiring and incorporating into our daily lives. By cultivating a daily gratitude practice you can experience more joy in your life, improve your relationships, reduce your stress, sleep better, experience fewer aches and pains, improve your immune system and feel more at peace. Those who list the things they are grateful for seem to have a brighter outlook on life.

Tips for experiencing gratitude:

❖ Keep a gratitude journal
❖ Write down the things you are grateful for daily
❖ Tell the people around you why you are thankful for them
❖ Serve others
❖ Stay in the present moment
❖ Be mindful
❖ Volunteer
❖ Recognize the little things
❖ Exercise
❖ Learn prayers of gratitude
❖ Give one compliment daily
❖ Choose not to complain
❖ Become involved in the things that are important to you

Clean Up Your Environment

Are you trying to get rid of the chemicals in your life? Are you reading labels, buying more natural products, and cleaning out your home of potentially dangerous toxins?

There may be more places than you thought where you can make changes, and get rid of potentially harmful chemicals in various areas of your life. Here are the top areas to focus on:

❖ Buy organic fruits and vegetables.

❖ If purchasing conventional produce, choose those considered to have the least amount of pesticide residue on them. These consist of:

- ◆ Asparagus
- ◆ Avocados
- ◆ Cabbage
- ◆ Cauliflower
- ◆ Eggplant
- ◆ Kiwi
- ◆ Onions
- ◆ Sweet Potatoes

> The average American is exposed to everything from food additives and preservatives to smog, exhaust and pollution, heavy metals, non-organic foods, pesticides, chemicals, and so much more.

❖ Either buy these organic or avoid:

- ◆ Apples
- ◆ Celery
- ◆ Cherry tomatoes
- ◆ Cucumbers
- ◆ Spinach
- ◆ Strawberries
- ◆ Bell peppers
- ◆ Hot peppers
- ◆ Kale/collard greens

❖ Ditch the BPA-free plastic storage containers and plastic water bottles for glass or stainless steel.

❖ Let go of the harsh, heavy-duty cleaners. These types of cleaners are simply too harmful to your body and the earth. Make the switch over to healthier versions or mix up your own.

❖ Take a hard look at your skin care products. Use organic, non-toxic skin care products without chemicals.

❖ Wash your hands with soap and water. Most hand sanitizers contain triclosan. If you must use hand sanitizers, look for triclosan-free versions. Triclosan is an antibacterial chemical agent added mainly to soaps, personal care and cleaning products. It's also found in clothing, cookware, furniture, flooring, toothpaste, toothbrushes, mattresses, shoe insoles, sponges and toys in an attempt to reduce bacteria levels. Triclosan has been shown to disrupt hormone regulation, disrupt immune system function and contribute to the development of antibiotic-resistant bacteria (i.e. superbugs).

❖ Use green plants as natural air detoxifiers. Spider plants, English Ivy, rubber plants and Boston ferns are some of the best for this purpose.

❖ Avoid GMOs.

Choose triclosan-free hand sanitizers...

What About Supplements?

Roby Mitchell, M.D. (Dr. Fitt) considers the below "Weapons of Mass Reduction" to be the most important supplements.

With the popularity of fast and inexpensive processed food, many of us struggle to get all the nutrients we need out of our diets. As a result, we often need to turn to supplements to do just that...supplement our diet.

Weapons of Mass Reduction

The Weapons of Mass Reduction are a fundamental group of supplements that will assist your efforts to re-establish normal metabolism (autonomic homeostasis). The basic reason we start to get fat and sick as we age is because there is a drop in metabolism, our ability to convert food into energy. The reduction in converting food to energy results in two primary conditions that lead to increased weight and sickness.

First, as we stop efficiently converting the blood sugar from our meals to energy, the sugar levels in our bloodstream start to rise. This is reflected in your blood work by a hemoglobin A1c (HgbA1c) above 5.2. HgbA1c measures how much sugar your red blood cells have acquired while traveling through your bloodstream. Since red blood cells live for about 90 days, the HgbA1c gives us a three-month reflection of blood sugar levels. This is a better test than the snapshot of a fasting blood sugar.

This constant excess sugar in your bloodstream stimulates the production of the primary fat storage hormone, insulin. Chronic overproduction of insulin causes fat storage, especially from the neck to the hips. We see midsections grow as people get past age 26. Insulin makes fat cells multiply. Once these fat cells are made, they then produce another fat storage hormone called "estrone." Estrone then multiplies the fat cell making process. Estrone is an estrogen. Estrone has more of an effect on tissues responsive to estrogens. This is why breast size increases in men and women with age.

The second condition that happens with a drop in metabolism is a rise in the level of critters in your body. Normally, we have 10 times as many bacteria in and on us as human cells. We also carry a load of viruses and fungi that outnumber the bacteria. One way we keep critter numbers under control is by producing body heat when we convert food to energy. When metabolism slows, energy production slows. When energy production goes down, so does body temperature. The effect is similar to what happens when food on the buffet line is not kept at the right temperature – we get critter overgrowth.

Critter overgrowth causes the immune system to react by producing chemicals called "cytokines." Cytokines are the chemicals produced by the immune system to kill critters. There are many types

> *Chronic inflammation is the common denominator in most Western diseases...*

of cytokines. Some cause fever, others cause runny noses, others cause redness and swelling. The symptoms you experience from the cold, flu and other viruses are actually not from the viruses but your immune system's response to the viruses. Normally, cytokine production is brief. Your immune system destroys the excess critters and cytokine production stops. However, if blood sugar levels stay elevated, critter levels are chronically elevated. This results in a long-term production of cytokines and the process called "inflammation." (Inflammation is derived from the Latin meaning "on fire.")

Chronic inflammation is the common denominator in most western diseases from Alzheimer's to heart disease to acne to autism to osteoporosis to autoimmune conditions. Cytokines are meant to destroy critters. However, long-term cytokine production also destroys normal cells/tissues. The joint destruction we see in rheumatoid arthritis is from cytokines. The cytokine leukotriene is the cause of asthma attacks. Cytokines can eat through artery walls in the heart or brain to produce a blood clot that causes a "heart attack" or stroke. Excess cytokine production causes many of the symptoms seen in autism. One group of cytokines are called "growth factors." Growth factors, like insulin and estrone, make fat cells multiply. Weight gain and obesity are also fueled by chronic inflammation.

The objectives of the Weapons of Mass Reduction are to increase metabolism and reduce critter levels. When this happens, insulin, estrone and growth factor levels go down. Weight loss becomes automatic and effortless when this is combined with the BALi Eating Plan®.

❖ *Eco Thyro* – Thyroid hormone is the hormone that acts like the spark plugs in your car. In your car carburetor, oxygen is combined with gasoline and a spark from the spark plugs to create energy. The same energy equation is used in your fireplace. Wood is the fuel and a match or lighter is the spark; together they create oxygen. Your body uses the same energy equation. Glucose replaces gasoline as the fuel. Burning up sugar for energy lowers blood sugar. It also creates heat. Higher body temperature means lower critter numbers. The TSH blood test checks your thyroid. Your TSH should be less than 1.0.

❖ *IodoRX* – IodoRX is a combination of iodiNe and iodiDe. These two minerals are in the same chemical class as chlorine-halogens. Halogens are powerful critter killers. This is why chlorine is in municipal water and public pools. Every cell in your body should be supplied with iodine or iodide in order to keep critter levels down. When man lived near the ocean, we got plenty of iodine. Today, most people don't get the amount of iodine needed for optimal health. If you have thyroid issues, replace iodine under medical supervision.

Oxygen + Fuel + Spark = Energy

❖ *B Complex 75* – B vitamins are critical to energy production. There are several B vitamins that work as a team. All must be present to facilitate converting glucose to energy. Menstruating women are especially prone to B complex deficiencies.

❖ *Magnesium Gel* – Your car creates energy two ways. One way is to burn gasoline. Another energy source is your car battery. Your car battery is filled with water and sectioned off into compartments called "cells." Electricity is created when electrolytes in the battery pass back and forth across the cell membranes. Movement of electrolytes is how batteries create energy in general. A similar thing happens in your body. Electrolytes flow back and forth across cells to create energy. Magnesium is an electrolyte associated with creating energy in humans. Magnesium gel is applied topically. This prevents the side effect of diarrhea from taking high levels of magnesium. This mechanism highlights the importance of staying hydrated. If water is inadequate in your body or your car battery, energy levels will suffer.

❖ *Selenium* – Selenium is a mineral that is critical for normal thyroid function. The thyroid hormone that is produced by the thyroid gland is thyroxine (T4). This molecule consists of the amino acid, tyrosine, with four molecules of iodine attached. This hormone then travels throughout the rest of the body and enters each cell to create energy. However, before it can effectively participate in the energy equation, one molecule of iodine must be removed to create triiodothyronine (T3). The conversion of T4 to T3 depends on an enzyme, selenomethionase. This enzyme is selenium dependent. If selenium levels are low, you won't efficiently convert T4 to T3. This is why many people don't do well with thyroid replacement using traditional synthetic T4 products. Use 400 mcg of selenium per day.

> *Magnesium is an electrolyte associated with creating energy*

❖ *Vitamin D3* – D3 actually turns out to be a hormone. One function of this hormone is to stimulate the immune cells to produce cathelicidins. Cathelicidins are natural critter killers produced by your immune cells. As sun exposure goes down in fall and winter, we make less vitamin D3 naturally. This is part of what leads to the cold/flu season. Vitamin D levels should be checked in blood work. Keep levels between 70 to 100.

❖ *Black seed oil* – Black seed oil is the ultimate critter killer. In 30 years of dealing with nutritional supplements, Dr. Mitchell has not seen anything as effective as black seed oil. The reason is the wide array of chemicals naturally occurring in this extract of black cumin seeds. In general, plants must have mechanisms that allow them to survive an environment filled with critters that want to eat them. As a defense, they create bark, peels, shells, husks or they create natural pesticides. The more potent and varied these natural critters are, the healthier they are for us. Black seed oil kills bacteria, viruses, fungi and parasites. There are light and dark varieties of black seed oil. The dark is more potent. Two tablespoons is a good maintenance dose of black seed oil. Increase the dose if you have more critters to get rid of. Black seed oil can also be used in ears, on pets and on skin to kill critters.

Combine the Weapons of Mass Reduction with the BALi Eating Plan® and you will see dramatic health improvements.

The Importance of Hydrochloric acid (HCL)

Hydrochloric acid is normally produced in response to every meal we eat. Hydrochloric acid acts like a meat tenderizer in breaking down proteins into their amino acid building blocks. Think of proteins as a strand of pearls with each pearl being an amino acid. If a protein is not totally broken down into individual amino acids, undigested proteins can

> *Black seed oil is the ultimate critter killer.*

make it into the bloodstream. This can cause an allergic reaction. A true allergy to one or two foods is not unlikely. However, if there are multiple food allergies, the problem is most likely insufficient production of hydrochloric acid. Hydrochloric acid levels decline with age but it's common for people to be born not producing enough. This is especially true for people whose mothers were over age 27 when they were born.

Hydrochloric acid also acts to sterilize everything we eat. Although you can't see them, everything you put into your mouth is covered with germs. When this food reaches the stomach, the stomach sprays it with hydrochloric acid to kill bacteria, viruses and fungi. Hydrochloric acid protects you from food poisoning. Hydrochloric acid also keeps down the population of Candida yeast, which normally resides in everyone's colon. If hydrochloric acid levels get low, bacteria and yeast overgrow and feed off the food you eat. This can cause symptoms such as heartburn,

reflux, excess gas/bloating, poor digestion, constipation, and other stomach problems. If the situation gets more serious due to a genetic predisposition, we see diseases such as irritable bowel, Crohn's, ulcerative colitis, and celiac disease. If yeast overgrows and is inhaled into the lungs, we see asthma. Yeast overgrowth can also weaken the immune system so that germs grow other places, such as the skin. Acne, eczema, and psoriasis are often due to low hydrochloric acid production. Additionally, the "good bacteria" in your gut, acidophilus, don't do well unless there is plenty of hydrochloric acid. (The name "acidophilus" means "acid loving.")

Hydrochloric acid is critical for the absorption of nutritional building blocks such as amino acids, vitamins and minerals. Vitamin B12, for instance, can't be absorbed unless there is adequate hydrochloric acid. A deficiency of vitamin B12 can lead to symptoms such as anemia, low energy, easy bruising/bleeding, bleeding gums, neuropathy (numbness/tingling) in hands/feet, depression, and memory loss that can be mistaken for Alzheimer's.

Amino acids are the building blocks of proteins. Hydrochloric acid breaks down proteins into individual amino acids. These amino acid building blocks can then be used to make other proteins needed by the body or other compound molecules needed for normal functioning. Healthy hair, skin and nails require adequate absorption of amino acids. Muscle and bones are made of protein. The antibodies that protect us from germs are made of protein. Chemicals made in the brain called "neurotransmitters" control our ability to think, remember, and control our moods. If you are not able to absorb amino acids because your hydrochloric acid levels are low, you may develop depression or other psychiatric disorders.

Homocysteine is an amino acid that is an important building block. However, if homocysteine levels get too high, this can lead to heart attacks, strokes, and Alzheimer's. The B vitamins: B12, B6, folate, and B1 are important to keep homocysteine levels normal. Normal homocysteine levels are more important than normal cholesterol levels in preventing strokes and heart attacks. Most doctors are unaware of this and do not check homocysteine levels. Your level should be 8 or below.

Work with your healthcare provider to determine the supplements that are right for you

BALi Testimonial

At 39 years old, I found myself closing in on 200 pounds. I had tried every fad diet and diet pill out there. I was exhausted all the time, my entire body hurt, and I had horrible brain fog. I was emotionally and spiritually bankrupt. I was just existing.

I committed to BALi eating and regular exercise. I have lost around 60 pounds and have kept it off for almost a year. I need less sleep because the quality of sleep I do get is so much better. I wake feeling rested and alert. For the first time in 20 years, I am not on any prescription medications.

Mentally, emotionally, and physically I feel better than I ever did in my 20s and 30s. Going BALi has given me my life back!

Missy Buchanan

Recipes

SAMPLE BALI DAILY MEAL PLAN

Breakfast:

Breakfast Stir Fry topped with Avocado

Lunch:

Kale Blueberry Salad

Afternoon snack:

Handful of raw nuts or seeds

Dinner:

Lemon & Garlic-Infused Salmon,
Spaghetti Squash
Sautéed Baby Kale

APPETIZERS & SNACKS

ALMOND BUTTER APPLE-WICH

Serves: 1

2 horizontal slices of green apple, cored
Almond butter
Granola

↪ Build your snack by layering almond butter and granola.

↪ This can be served open-faced or as an apple-wich. Enjoy!

Notes:

APPLE PIE MASON JAR OATMEAL

½ cup rolled oats (not instant)
¾ cup unsweetened almond milk
1 teaspoon ground cinnamon
½ teaspoon vanilla extract
Dash of nutmeg
¼ cup unsweetened applesauce
1 teaspoon chia seeds
1 teaspoon pure maple syrup or raw honey to taste

This is another great option for busy individuals, and it can be doubled or tripled, so you have them in your refrigerator to grab and go!

❧ Combine all ingredients in a Mason jar or storage container.

❧ Place in the refrigerator and enjoy the next day.

Notes:

BLACK BEAN AVOCADO BOWL

Serves: 4-6

1 can black beans, drained and rinsed

1 avocado, diced

2 green onions, diced

1 tomato, diced

1 small cucumber, diced

1 cup chopped pepper (red, yellow and/or orange)

2 minced garlic cloves

1 jalapeno, seeded and diced

Cilantro to taste

Lime juice to taste

↩ Mix all together.

↩ Refrigerate for an hour for increased flavor.

Notes:

BLUEBERRY CHIA PUDDING

Serves: 2

1 cup unsweetened almond milk

3 tablespoons chia seeds

1½ tablespoons unsweetened shredded coconut

½ tablespoon pure maple syrup

½ teaspoon vanilla extract

½ cup blueberries

Optional: Top with almond slices

Add all ingredients to a container, except almonds, and stir. Put a lid on the container and place it in the refrigerator overnight.

Serve topped with optional almond slices.

Notes:

BLUEBERRY YOGURT PARFAIT

Serves: 2

1 cup plain Greek yogurt

½ cup granola (see homemade recipe)

½ cup blueberries (any berry can be used)

¼ cup raw walnuts (or other nuts)

1 tablespoon raw honey

⅛ teaspoon vanilla extract

¼ teaspoon cinnamon

Combine yogurt, granola, blueberries and walnuts. Enjoy.

Notes:

CAPRESE DELUXE

1 large tomato, sliced
1 avocado, sliced
¼ cup feta or goat cheese (optional)
Balsamic vinegar to taste
Extra virgin olive oil
Sea salt and black pepper to taste

⇗ Compile one slice tomato, one slice avocado, optional feta or goat cheese, then repeat until have used all of the tomatoes, avocado and feta.

⇗ Drizzle with balsamic vinegar and olive oil. Serve immediately.

Notes:

Garden Salsa with Spelt Tortilla Chips *pages 90 & 100*

...never have to worry about weighing anything or counting calories, carbs, proteins, or fats.

Sweet Potato Chips *page 101*

Cucumber Hummus Cups *page 88*

CUCUMBER HUMMUS CUPS

1 container prepared hummus
2 cucumbers, partially peeled
Paprika

꿴 Cut cucumbers into $\frac{1}{2}$-inch thick slices and scoop out seeds with a melon baller or a small spoon, leaving bottom intact to form a cup.

꿴 Fill each with hummus, sprinkle with paprika and serve.

Notes:

ELLIE'S QUICK & ZESTY BEAN DIP

Makes approximately 2 cups

16-ounce can refried beans
½ cup organic salsa
1 tablespoon lime juice
1 teaspoon dried cilantro
1 to 2 teaspoons ground cumin
1 teaspoon hot sauce (to taste)
1 teaspoon chili powder
Carrot sticks, pepper strips, black bean chips

❧ Place all ingredients in a bowl and mix well with a spoon. Enjoy!

Notes:

GARDEN SALSA

1 orange bell pepper, seeded and diced
1 yellow bell pepper, seeded and diced
1 red bell pepper, seeded and diced
1 avocado, peeled, pitted and diced
1 jalapeno, seeded and diced
1 pound tomatoes, seeded and diced
½ red onion, diced
¼ cup fresh chopped cilantro
½ teaspoon cumin
½ teaspoon sea salt
Juice of 1 lime

☙ Combine all ingredients together in a bowl.

☙ Stir until combined.

Notes:

GUACAMOLE

Serves: 4-6

3 perfectly ripe avocados
½ shallot, chopped fine
1 small jalapeno, ribs and seeds removed, diced*
Juice ½ lime
1 clove garlic, minced
Sea salt and black pepper to taste

Note: For spicier guacamole, only remove half of the ribs and seeds.

In a medium bowl, add the avocado, shallots, jalapeno, lime juice and garlic.

Mash with a fork to desired texture (we prefer it a little chunky).

Add salt and pepper to taste. If you are serving with chips, be conservative on the salt since there will be salt in the chips. Enjoy!

Notes:

HOMEMADE GRANOLA

Makes approximately 4 cups

3 cups rolled oats (not instant)
2 tablespoons molasses (optional)
½ teaspoon ground cinnamon
¼ teaspoon sea salt
⅓ cup raw honey
¼ cup extra virgin olive oil
1 teaspoon vanilla extract
¼ to ½ cup currants
½ cup coarsely chopped raw or toasted nuts or seeds

Homemade granola is easy to make and customize to your preferences.

◦ Preheat oven to 300° F.

◦ In a medium bowl, combine the oats, molasses, cinnamon and salt.

◦ In a small bowl, mix together the honey, olive oil and vanilla. Gradually add to the dry mix until the oats are completely coated.

◦ Spread the mixture in a thin, even layer on a rimmed baking sheet. Bake for 15 minutes, then stir and continue baking until the granola is very light golden brown, (about 5 to 15 more minutes). Remove from the oven and let cool for about 20 minutes.

◦ Add currants, nuts and seeds and/or anything else you desire. Once completely cooled, store in an airtight jar.

Notes:

MASON JAR BLUEBERRY OATMEAL

Serves: 1

½ cup rolled oats (not instant)
¾ cup unsweetened almond milk
½ cup blueberries
1 tablespoon chopped, raw walnuts
1 teaspoon raw honey or a few drops stevia
1 tablespoon ground flaxseeds

This is a great option for busy individuals. It is perfect for a quick breakfast, lunch or snack on the go. It can be eaten hot or cold. Use a half-pint (1 cup) Mason jar for the perfect serving size. This recipe can be doubled or tripled, so you have them in your refrigerator to grab and go!

~ Combine all ingredients in a storage container.

~ Place in the refrigerator and enjoy the next day.

Notes:

NO-BAKE ENERGY BITES

1 cup rolled oats (not instant)
½ cup almond butter
½ cup ground flaxseeds
⅓ cup raw honey
1 teaspoon vanilla extract

☙ Combine all ingredients.

☙ Place in refrigerator for 30 minutes, and then roll into balls. Store balls in refrigerator or freezer.

Notes:

NUTTY GRANOLA BARS

Makes approximately 18 bars

7 cups rolled oats (not instant)
½ cup olive oil
1 teaspoon sea salt
¾ cup raw honey
¼ cup molasses
1 tablespoon vanilla extract
2 to 3 teaspoons ground cinnamon
Dash nutmeg
1½ cup raw walnuts, chopped
½ cup raw almonds, chopped

Notes:

_____

_____

_____

✒ Preheat oven to 375° F. Line a cookie sheet with parchment paper.

✒ In a large bowl, combine the oats, oil, and salt until oats are evenly coated. Transfer to cookie sheet and spread out. Bake for 20 to 25 minutes, stirring every 5 minutes.

✒ Remove the oats. Lower the oven temperature to 300° F.

✒ In the large bowl, combine the honey, molasses, vanilla, cinnamon, nutmeg, walnuts, almonds and oats. Stir until everything is evenly coated.

✒ Spray the parchment paper in the pan with coconut oil. Transfer the oats mixture to the cookie sheet and spread out evenly. Firmly press the mixture into the pan. Bake until golden, about 35 to 40 min.

✒ Cool for 15 minutes, then cut the bars. If you wait longer than 15 minutes, they will be hard and crumbly when you try to cut them. These can be stored in an air-tight container or frozen for future use.

You don't have to eat less; you just have to eat right.

Guacamole *page 91*

Mason Jar Blueberry Oatmeal *page 93*

Sweet Potato Skins *page 102*

PURPLE KALE CHIPS

Serves: 3-4

1 bunch purple kale
2 tablespoons olive oil
Sea salt

ﾐ Preheat oven to 300° F.

ﾐ Trim an inch off the ends of the stems. Drizzle kale with olive oil and toss to coat. Sprinkle with salt.

ﾐ Place kale on a cookie sheet and bake for 15 minutes, turning once.

Notes:

ROASTED CHICKPEAS

1 can chickpeas, drained and rinsed
1 tablespoon extra virgin olive oil
1 teaspoon dried oregano
Sea salt and black pepper to taste

🍃 Preheat oven to 350° F.

🍃 Combine all ingredients in a bowl and blend well.

🍃 Spread into one layer on a cookie sheet.

🍃 Bake 15 to 45 minutes depending on if you want them soft or crunchy. Stir halfway through cooking.

Notes: Feel free to add any other dried herbs and spices. You could also roast a package of grape tomatoes with the chickpea mixture. These can be eaten by themselves or added to salads.

Notes:

ROASTED NUTS

Makes 7 cups

1 cup raw almonds
1 cup raw walnuts
1 cup raw cashews
1 cup pistachios, shelled
1 cup raw pecans
1 cup raw hazel nuts
1 cup raw Brazil nuts
2 tablespoons extra virgin olive oil
2 tablespoons sesame oil
Sea salt to taste
Bragg herbs to taste*
Cayenne pepper to taste (optional)

* See Appendix A for Resources

↩ Preheat oven to 350° F.

↩ Place the nuts in a bowl and combine with olive oil, sesame oil, salt, Braggs herbs and cayenne pepper (optional). Let sit for 15 to 20 minutes for the nuts to absorb the seasoning.

↩ Spread out on a large baking sheet and cook for 10 minutes. Stir and then cook for another 5 minutes.

Notes:

_____

_____

_____

SPELT TORTILLA CHIPS

Serves: 3

4 BALi-friendly tortillas, cut into tortilla chip size*
2 tablespoons extra virgin olive oil
Sea salt and black pepper to taste, divided

* See recipes to make your own tortillas or buy BALi-friendly tortillas. See Appendix A for resources.

These are delicious with the Simply BALi Garden Salsa recipe and Guacamole recipe.

❧ Preheat oven to 375° F.

❧ Brush tortilla slices with olive oil, then place them on a baking sheet.

❧ Top with salt. Bake until crisp.

Notes:

SWEET POTATO CHIPS

Serves: 3-4

2 large sweet potatoes
2 tablespoons melted coconut oil
2 teaspoons dried rosemary
1 teaspoon sea salt

๛ Preheat oven to 375°F.

๛ Thinly slice sweet potatoes. In a large bowl, toss sweet potatoes with coconut oil, rosemary, and salt.

๛ Place sweet potato chips in a single layer on a baking sheet covered with parchment paper. Bake for 10 minutes, then flip the chips over and bake for another 10 minutes. For the last 10 minutes, watch the chips closely and pull off any chips that start to brown, until all of the chips are cooked. YUM!

Notes:

SWEET POTATO SKINS

3 sweet potatoes
1 tablespoon coconut oil, gently melted
Sea salt and black pepper to taste
24 grape tomatoes, quartered
Guacamole*

Note: You can either use fresh, pre-made guacamole or make your own.

❧ Preheat oven to 375° F.

❧ Bake sweet potatoes for 1 hour.

❧ When the potatoes are done, increase the oven temperature to 450° F. Cut the potatoes in half and scoop out some of the middle (being careful not to burn yourself). Top each half with gently melted coconut oil, salt and pepper.

❧ Bake until the edges of the sweet potato begin to brown a little, about 10 to 14 minutes.

❧ Top with tomatoes and guacamole. Serve!

Notes:

HEALTHY SNACK OPTIONS

☐ Almond butter
☐ Almonds, raw and unsalted
☐ Avocado
☐ Beanitos chips
☐ Beef jerky, grass-fed
☐ Blackberries
☐ Blueberries
☐ Broccoli
☐ Cauliflower
☐ Celery
☐ Cherry tomatoes
☐ Chicken salad
☐ Chopped veggies with hummus
☐ Crackers and almond butter packets
☐ Cucumbers
☐ Dark chocolate (at least 70%)
☐ Egg muffins
☐ Egg salad
☐ Energy bites
☐ Green apple
☐ Green peppers
☐ Guacamole
☐ Hard-boiled eggs
☐ Homemade pizza

☐ Hummus
☐ Kale chips
☐ Leftovers
☐ Oatmeal bars
☐ Oatmeal jars
☐ Olives
☐ Pecans, raw and unsalted
☐ Pistachios
☐ Pumpkin seeds, raw and unsalted
☐ Purple carrots
☐ Roasted chickpeas
☐ Salad jars
☐ Salsa
☐ Soup
☐ Strawberries
☐ Sunflower seeds
☐ Sweet potato chips, made with coconut oil
☐ Trail mix
☐ Tuna salad
☐ Turkey breast, nitrate free
☐ Walnuts, raw and unsalted
☐ Yogurt
☐ Zucchini

BALi Testimonial

When I hit my late 30s, I noticed that I could no longer eat what I wanted without gaining weight. I tried every gimmick imaginable and never had success with weight loss. I exercised and thought I was eating healthy.

As I hit my 40s, I was tired, depressed, and gaining weight at a rate I was very unhappy about. I posted something on Facebook one day about my feelings of fatness, depression, no energy, etc. A friend replied and told me about Roby Mitchell, M.D. and the BALi lifestyle.

I'm a nurse practitioner and every day one of my patients asks me about weight loss. Up until about a year ago, I had no idea what to tell people. Sure I could prescribe a weight loss drug, but they truly are not effective. So my friend, Julie Hulsey, "hooked" me up with Roby Mitchell, M.D.

I did the Weight is Over Class and lost 17 pounds, continued my BALi journey and have lost several more pounds, I am no longer tired, depressed, and I have tons of energy. I have helped many people change their lives and become healthy. The BALi way of life is simple and effective. I have never felt better!

Amy Dunn,
Nurse Practitioner

BREAKFAST, LUNCH & DINNER

ALL-IN-ONE WRAP

Serves: 1

1 cup spinach
1 tablespoon extra virgin olive oil
1 organic, free-range egg
1 BALi-friendly tortilla*
2 slices turkey
½ avocado, mashed

Optional Dressing:
¼ cup plain yogurt
1 teaspoon stone ground mustard
1 drop raw honey
Sea salt and black pepper to taste

* See recipes to make your own tortillas or buy BALi-friendly tortillas. See Appendix A for resources.

~ Prepare optional dressing by combining all dressing ingredients. Set aside.

~ Add oil and spinach to medium pan and sauté over medium heat until slightly wilted. Set aside in bowl.

~ Cook egg in pan, then set aside.

~ Top tortilla with turkey slices, spinach, egg and avocado. Fold the sides in and roll. Top with optional dressing.

Notes:

ANNA'S NUTTY BLENDER PANCAKES

Serves: 4

1½ cups rolled oats (not instant)
¾ cup unsweetened almond milk
2 tablespoons raw honey
3 tablespoons almond butter
2 tablespoons ground flaxseed
1 teaspoon aluminum-free baking powder
½ teaspoon vanilla extract

≈ Add oats and almond milk to a blender and blend until thoroughly mixed.

≈ Add in remaining ingredients and blend again.

≈ Cook as you would any pancake mix.

Simply BALi *Tip: For a protein boost, you can add 1-2 servings of BALi whey protein powder. You may need to increase your liquid slightly to offset the dry ingredients.*

Notes:

AVOCADO SALSA BOWL

Serves: 2

1 avocado, pitted
Sea salt
2 lime wedges
3 tablespoons fresh salsa
¼ cup black beans, drained

&⤳ Season the avocado halves with a little salt. Squeeze limes over the avocados.

&⤳ In a bowl, combine the salsa and beans.

&⤳ Divide the mixture between the avocados. Serve!

Notes:

BACON-TOPPED MEATLOAF

Serves: 4-6

1 tablespoon chili powder

1/4 teaspoon each: garlic powder, sea salt, ground black pepper

1/8 teaspoon each: cayenne pepper, turmeric, onion powder

1 pound grass-fed ground beef

1 pound ground turkey

8-ounce can of organic tomato sauce, divided

1 large free-range egg, beaten

1/4 to 1/2 cup of chia seeds

1/3 cup chopped onion

2/3 cup black beans, drained and rinsed

14-ounce container organic diced tomatoes

1/2 cup organic shredded jack cheese (optional)

1/2 cup organic shredded cheddar cheese (optional)

3 strips bacon (without nitrates)

Notes:

_____

_____

_____

~ Preheat oven to 375° F.

~ In a medium bowl, mix chili powder, garlic powder, salt, black pepper, cayenne pepper, turmeric, and onion powder. Then, combine with turkey and beef.

~ In medium bowl, mix half the can of tomato sauce, egg and chia seeds. Let sit for 5+ minutes to allow the chia seeds to absorb the liquid. Add to meat mixture.

~ Using the same bowl, combine onion, beans and tomatoes. Set aside.

~ On a piece of waxed paper flatten out the meat to about a 1/2 to 1-inch thick, cut in half. Place half in a greased 8 x 8-inch pan. Top that half with the onion/bean/tomato mixture and optional cheese.

~ Take the second half of the flattened meat and place on top of the other half. Press the sides together to seal. Top the loaf with the other half of the tomato sauce and the bacon.

~ Bake for 35 to 40 minutes. Let set for about 10 minutes before slicing.

BLACK BEAN BURGER

Serves: 4-6

1 sweet potato, cut into 1-inch chunks
(approximately 1 cup)
3 tablespoons coconut oil, divided
Pinch sea salt
½ cup red onion, finely diced
16-ounce can black beans, rinsed and drained
1 cup cooked black rice
2 cloves garlic, minced
½ tablespoon ground cumin
1 teaspoon chili powder
½ teaspoon sea salt
3 tablespoons tamari
2 teaspoons Bragg Liquid Aminos
⅛ cup breadcrumbs or almond meal

Notes:

🌿 Preheat oven to 425° F. Line a small baking sheet with parchment paper.

🌿 In a medium bowl, combine the potato, 1 tablespoon gently melted coconut oil and salt. Spread the potatoes onto the pan and roast for 20 to 25 minutes or until tender, stirring frequently.

🌿 In a small pan, sauté a tablespoon of coconut oil and red onion for 5 minutes.

🌿 In a food processor, pulse the remaining ingredients together with the roasted potatoes and onion, being careful not to over mix. Cool in the refrigerator, so you can form 6 patties.

🌿 In a large skillet, add 1 tablespoon melted coconut oil and patties. Brown on both sides over medium heat.

🌿 Serve topped with your favorite toppings: lettuce, tomato, onion and/or guacamole.

BREAKFAST IN A PAN

> **Serves: 1**

1 BALi-friendly tortilla
½ cup black refried beans
¼ cup fresh tomatoes, sliced
6 asparagus stalks
1 organic, free-range egg
Sea salt and black pepper to taste

* See recipes to make your own tortillas or buy BALi-friendly tortillas. See Appendix A for resources.

↬ Preheat oven to 350° F.

↬ Place tortilla in the bottom of a round, greased baking or cast iron pan.

↬ Top with refried beans, tomatoes, asparagus, egg, salt and pepper.

↬ Bake until the egg is cooked to your liking (approximately 12 to 15 minutes).

Notes:

BREAKFAST STIR FRY

Serves: 4

2 tablespoons coconut oil
1 pound chicken, cooked, cut into strips
2 cups broccoli slaw
10 Brussels sprouts, trimmed and chopped
½ medium red onion, diced
4 garlic cloves, diced
2 cups zucchini, chopped
3 cups mixed greens, cut into ribbons
1 cup guacamole

Combine coconut oil, chicken, broccoli slaw, Brussels sprouts, red onion and garlic in a large pan. Sauté over medium heat until the vegetables have softened, about 10 to 12 minutes.

Add zucchini and mixed greens; sauté for another minute.

Move to serving plates and top with guacamole.

Notes:

BRIAN'S FAMOUS BURRITOS

Serves: 4-6

2 tablespoons coconut oil

1 red onion, chopped

1 pound grass-fed ground beef (90/10)

1 cup black refried beans

15-ounce can organic diced tomatoes (do not drain)

1 cup leftover black rice (optional)

¼ teaspoon cumin

¼ teaspoon chili powder

¼ teaspoon garlic powder

⅛ teaspoon oregano

2 tablespoons cilantro

⅛ teaspoon sea salt

¼ teaspoon black pepper

8-ounce can tomato sauce

4 to 6 BALi-friendly tortillas*

½ cup organic, shredded cheddar cheese

1 cup organic plain Greek yogurt

Notes:

↝ In a large skillet, melt the coconut oil over medium heat.

↝ Add the onion and cook for 3 to 4 minutes or until softened.

↝ Add ground beef and cook until browned.

↝ Add refried beans, black rice (optional) and diced tomatoes; heat through.

↝ Add cumin, garlic, oregano, cilantro, salt, and pepper.

↝ Add tomato sauce. You can add a little water if mix is too dry. Simmer for 5 minutes. Add mixture to tortillas and sprinkle with cheddar cheese. Fold over the ends of the tortilla and then roll them up. Top with Greek yogurt.

↝ These can be placed in the oven without the yogurt at 170° F to keep warm until ready to serve. You can also wrap them in parchment paper and then foil and freeze for later.

See recipes to make your own tortillas or buy BALi-friendly tortillas. See Appendix A for resources.

CHICKEN CURRY WITH WINTER VEGETABLES

Serves: 6-8

2 tablespoons coconut oil

1 onion, peeled and diced

1 tablespoon curry powder

1 medium squash, seeded and cut into 1-inch squares

1 medium celery root, peeled and chopped

Small handful of Brussels sprouts, halved

15-ounce can garbanzo beans, drained and rinsed

1 cup shredded chicken (optional)

13.5-ounce can full-fat, unsweetened, organic coconut milk

4 cups low sodium vegetable broth

1 bunch greens (kale, bok choy, collards, or turnip greens), washed, cut

Sea salt and black pepper to taste

Time Saving Tip – Butternut squash is available in the produce section already cut. You can use one container pre-cut squash.

Notes:

❧ In a large pot heat coconut oil and sauté onions and curry spices until the onions are soft (about 6 to 8 minutes).

❧ Add the vegetables, beans, chicken, coconut milk and vegetable stock. Simmer until the squash is tender (about 15 minutes). Add the greens, and then season with salt and pepper.

❧ Serve by itself or over black rice.

Freeze leftovers.

CHICKEN FAJITAS

Serves: 4

2 tablespoons olive oil

2 teaspoons chili powder

2 teaspoons cumin

½ teaspoon garlic powder

½ teaspoon oregano

¼ teaspoon sea salt

15-ounce can diced tomatoes

1 pound boneless chicken breasts or thighs, cut into strips

1 bag frozen, organic fajita blend (peppers and onions)

4 BALi-friendly tortillas*

Optional toppings: lettuce, guacamole, medium or hot salsa, cheese

See recipes to make your own tortillas or buy BALi-friendly tortillas. See Appendix A for resources.

This is a quick and easy, healthy dinner for those busy nights. It can even be assembled in the morning, so it is ready for the oven when you walk in the door at night.

❧ Preheat oven to 400° F.

❧ In a large bowl combine the oil, chili powder, cumin, garlic powder, oregano and salt. Then, add the tomatoes and chicken.

❧ Thaw the fajita blend in a colander under warm water, then add to the bowl. Stir to combine.

❧ Add the mixture to a 13 x 9-inch baking dish and bake until the chicken is thoroughly cooked and the vegetables are tender, about 20 minutes. Serve over mixed greens or on tortillas with optional toppings.

Notes:

CHICKEN LETTUCE WRAPS WITH CILANTRO DRESSING

Serves: 2-3

2 tablespoons fresh lime juice (about 1 large lime)

2 tablespoons minced fresh cilantro leaves

¼ to ½ teaspoon red pepper flakes

½ teaspoon raw honey

1 cup cooked chicken, shredded (approximately 6 ounces)

½ cup canned black beans, drained and rinsed

1 carrot (peeled and shredded) or 1 cup pre-made shredded carrots

½ cup organic salsa

4 butter lettuce, cabbage or romaine leaves

½ cup diced avocado

♆ Combine lime juice, cilantro, red pepper flakes and honey in a small bowl.

♆ Warm chicken, beans, carrots, salsa and cilantro in a large skillet. Once heated, spoon filling evenly into 4 lettuce leaves and top with avocado and lime juice mixture.

Notes:

COLORFUL SCRAMBLED EGG PLATE

2 teaspoons coconut oil, divided
2 organic, free-range eggs
2 cups fresh spinach, chopped
¼ cup black beans, rinsed and drained
¼ cup cherry tomatoes, halved
¼ cup orange bell pepper
Sea salt and black pepper to taste
1 BALi-friendly tortilla* (optional)

See recipes to make your own tortillas or buy BALi-friendly tortillas. See Appendix A for resources.

⮑ Heat a small pan over medium heat and add 1 teaspoon coconut oil.

⮑ While the pan is heating, add 2 eggs to a bowl and use a wire whisk to combine.

⮑ Add eggs to heated pan and cook, stirring constantly until cooked through.

⮑ In another small pan, add 1 teaspoon coconut oil and heat over medium low heat. Add the beans and peppers to the pan. Once heated though, add spinach and tomatoes cooking until slightly wilted.

⮑ Put all ingredients on a plate and season with salt and pepper. Serve with optional tortilla on the side.

Notes:

Avocado Salsa Bowl *page 109*

"The fork is your most powerful tool to change your health and the planet; food is the most powerful medicine to heal chronic illness."

– Mark Hyman, M.D.>

Ground Turkey & Veggies *page 128*

Loaded Sweet Potato with Chicken *page 135*

CROCK-POT PORK ROAST

⅓ cup low sodium chicken or vegetable broth
⅓ cup balsamic vinegar
1 tablespoon Bragg Liquid Aminos
1 tablespoon raw honey
2-pound boneless pork shoulder roast (sirloin roast)
½ teaspoon garlic powder
½ teaspoon red pepper flakes
Sea salt, to taste

↩ In a small bowl, combine the broth, vinegar, liquid aminos and honey.

↩ Place your roast into the crock-pot. Pour the broth mixture over the roast. Sprinkle garlic powder, red pepper flakes and salt over the roast.

↩ Cook for 4 hours on high or 6 to 8 hours on low.

Notes:

EASY CROCK-POT ROAST CHICKEN

Serves: 4

1 whole chicken, giblets removed
(approximately 4 pounds)
2 teaspoons paprika
1 teaspoon onion powder
1 teaspoon garlic powder
1 teaspoon thyme
1 teaspoon sea salt
¼ teaspoon black pepper
¼ teaspoon cayenne pepper

↝ Unwrap chicken, remove giblets and place it in the crock-pot.

↝ Top with each of the seasonings, covering as much surface area as possible.

↝ Cook on high in crock-pot for approximately 4 hours or low for approximately 8 hours. Check the temperature to ensure the chicken is done prior to serving. Enjoy!

Note: Use the seasonings and bones to make your own easy chicken broth. See the recipe in the Soups & Stews section.

Notes:

EASY 5 MINUTE GREENS & GARBANZO BEANS

1 can garbanzo beans, drained and rinsed
½ cup or more medium organic salsa to taste
2 handfuls of spring greens
Guacamole

🍃 In medium saucepan, combine garbanzo beans, spring greens and salsa until warm and greens slightly wilted.

🍃 Top each serving with half of the guacamole packet.

Notes:

EGG MUFFINS

Makes 12 muffins

Coconut oil spray

12-ounce cooked sausage or 8-ounce cooked bacon, crumbled (uncured and without nitrates)

1 tablespoon extra virgin olive oil

1 red bell pepper, diced

¼ large red onion, diced

1 cup spinach, cut into ribbons

3 tablespoons fresh basil leaves, cut into ribbons (optional)

10 organic, free-range eggs

½ teaspoon minced garlic

¼ teaspoon sea salt

¼ teaspoon black pepper

Pinch red pepper flakes

Notes:

These muffins can be cooked ahead and eaten throughout the week. They can also be frozen and reheated when you are ready to eat them.

❧ Preheat your oven to 350° F. Grease a 12-cup muffin tin with coconut oil spray.

❧ Chop the sausage or bacon into bite-size pieces.

❧ In a large skillet, heat the olive oil over medium heat. Sauté the sausage/bacon, peppers and onions until they begin to soften, about 3 minutes. Turn off the heat and stir in spinach and optional basil. Spoon the meat and veggie mixture into the muffin pan.

❧ In a large bowl, combine the eggs with the garlic, salt, pepper and red pepper flakes. Scramble and pour over the meat and veggies. Bake for 25 minutes, or until they puff up and feel slightly firm to the touch.

EGGS OVER PURPLE POTATO HOME FRIES

Serves: 1

1 tablespoon coconut oil
¼ medium red onion, diced
3 small purple potatoes, diced
¼ cup green peppers, diced
2 cloves fresh garlic, diced
¼ cup shiitake mushrooms, diced
Cayenne pepper, optional
Sea salt and black pepper to taste
2 organic, free-range eggs

Add oil, onion, potatoes, peppers, and garlic to a small pan over medium heat. Sauté until potatoes have cooked and vegetables have softened. Add mushrooms and heat through for 1 to 2 minutes. Season with cayenne pepper, salt and black pepper, remove from pan and set aside.

Add eggs to pan and cook over medium heat until cooked to desired doneness, then flip. Remove from pan when done.

Place potatoes on a plate and top with eggs.

Notes:

FETA CHICKEN WITH LENTILS & BROCCOLI

Serves: 2

2 cups black lentils, uncooked
1 cup low sodium vegetable broth
1 cup water
2 chicken breasts
Bragg Organic Sprinkle Seasoning
½ cup feta cheese (optional)
2 cups fresh broccoli, chopped
2 tablespoons ghee, divided
1 cup cherry tomatoes, quartered
2 teaspoons sesame seeds
Sea salt and pepper to taste

↝ Preheat oven to 350° F

↝ Add lentils, broth and water to pan. Cook until done. Add more water if necessary.

↝ Place chicken breasts on a baking sheet. Season with Bragg seasoning. Bake until chicken is done, topping with optional feta cheese the last few minutes of cooking.

↝ Steam broccoli in a steamer basket on the stove until desired doneness.

↝ When lentils and broccoli are done, **combine** them together, along with ghee **tomatoes,** sesame seeds, salt and pepper.

Notes:

FETA, MUSHROOM, & KALE OMELET

Serves: 1

2 teaspoons coconut oil
¼ medium red onion, diced
1 cup kale, stemmed, sliced
¼ cup shiitake mushrooms
2 organic, free-range eggs
4 green olives, diced
2 tablespoons feta cheese
½ avocado, sliced
¼ lemon, sliced
Sea salt and black pepper to taste

❧ Heat a small pan over medium heat and add coconut oil. Add onion and sauté for 4 minutes. Then, add kale and mushrooms and sauté until slightly wilted and onions are translucent. Set aside vegetables in a bowl.

❧ In another bowl, scramble eggs with a fork, then add the eggs to the pan. Cook until the eggs have set.

❧ Then, flip the egg over and cook for 3 minutes. Add the vegetables to one side of the eggs, top with cheese and fold over. Cook until the cheese has melted. Add salt to taste.

❧ Serve with sliced avocado and top with fresh lemon juice, salt and pepper.

Notes:

FRIED EGGPLANT

Serves: 2

1 eggplant, washed and sliced
2 to 3 organic, free-range eggs (depending on the size of your eggplant)
3 tablespoons olive oil
2 cloves garlic, chopped
1 cup shredded Parmesan cheese (optional)
Juice of one lemon
Sea salt and black pepper

Fried eggplant is so easy and very, very yummy!

∼ Place eggplant slices on parchment paper and sprinkle both sides with salt. Let them sit for 15 minutes or until the eggplant "sweats." Pat eggplant with a paper towel.

∼ Preheat oven to 350° F.

∼ Beat eggs with a fork in a bowl.

∼ Heat a sauté pan over medium heat. Add olive oil and garlic. Dip slices of eggplant in the egg and then place in a heated pan. Brown each side.

∼ When done, place the eggplant on a cookie sheet. Sprinkle each plant slice with Parmesan cheese and cook for 12 to 15 minutes or until cheese is golden brown.

∼ Remove from oven, squeeze fresh lemon juice over them and season with salt and pepper.

Notes:

GROUND TURKEY & VEGGIES

1 tablespoon coconut oil

1 pound ground turkey

3 cups of vegetables (bell peppers, zucchini, tomatoes, broccoli slaw, Brussels sprouts, yellow squash, etc.)

½ medium red onion, diced

2 garlic cloves, minced

1 teaspoon ground cumin

1 teaspoon ground coriander

1 teaspoon fennel seeds

¼ cup parsley, chopped

½ teaspoon sea salt

Black pepper to taste

❧ Place coconut oil, vegetables, onion, garlic, cumin, coriander, fennel and salt in a large pan. Sauté until the meat is no longer pink and the vegetables are tender.

❧ Stir in parsley and black pepper to taste. Serve by itself, over mixed greens, or topped with guacamole.

Notes:

GROUND TURKEY TACOS

Serves: 4

1 pound ground turkey
1 can Eden Organic black beans, drained
½ cup filtered water
1 tablespoon chili powder
½ teaspoon garlic powder
½ teaspoon onion powder
⅛ teaspoon red pepper flakes
¼ teaspoon dried oregano
½ teaspoon paprika
1½ teaspoons ground cumin
1 teaspoon sea salt
1 teaspoon black pepper
¼ teaspoon toasted, ground black cumin seeds (optional)

Optional toppings:
~ Guacamole
~ Cherry tomatoes, halved or quartered
~ Spinach, cut into ribbons
~ Organic salsa
~ Cheese

In a medium pan, cook the ground turkey.

Add remaining ingredients and cook on low heat until water is absorbed.

Drain grease.

Serve with tortillas or over a bed of lettuce. Top with optional toppings.

Notes:
_____
_____
_____
_____

HOT SAUSAGE & VEGGIE STIR FRY

Serves: 4

1 tablespoon coconut oil

2 carrots (unpeeled), cut into strips

2 celery stalks, cut into strips

1 medium red onion, cut into strips

2 green peppers, cut into strips

¾ cup organic, low sodium vegetable broth

1 package of nitrate-free hot sausage

2 small to medium zucchini (skin on), cut into strips

½ cup mushrooms (more if you'd like), sliced

2 tablespoons coconut aminos

¼ teaspoon sea salt

¼ teaspoon black pepper

Time-Saving Tip: Use pre-shredded carrots and slaw

Notes:

Stir-fries are quick, easy, and nutritional meals. Be creative when selecting these recipes. You do not have to follow them exactly. Use what you have. Replace the vegetables that you don't like and add in other vegetables. Feel free to throw in chicken, ground beef, ground turkey, steak, pork, fish, shrimp, liver, bacon or sausage. You can serve the stir-fry over black/red rice, quinoa, soba noodles or in BALi-approved tortillas. Double your recipe and you will have leftovers for the following day.

~ Heat the coconut oil in a large skillet.

~ Add carrots and celery, cook for 3 to 4 minutes.

~ Add the onion, green peppers, broth and sausage. Cook for another 3 to 4 minutes.

~ Add the zucchini and cook for 2 to 3 minutes. Add the mushrooms, coconut aminos, salt and black pepper and serve.

LEMON & GARLIC-INFUSED SALMON, SPAGHETTI SQUASH & SAUTÉED BABY KALE

Serves: 2

1 small spaghetti squash

4 tablespoons sesame oil, divided

4 cloves garlic, chopped, divided

2 lemons, divided

Sea salt, black pepper and cayenne pepper to taste, divided

½ pound Alaskan salmon

3 cups baby kale

2 tablespoons and 1 teaspoon grass-fed, organic butter or olive oil, divided

Notes:

⁌ Preheat oven to 400° F.

⁌ Cut spaghetti squash in half, remove seeds and place on baking sheet. Rub 2 tablespoons sesame oil on the inside of the squash. Squeeze half of one lemon over spaghetti squash halves. Top with 1 clove chopped garlic and season with salt, black pepper and cayenne pepper. Bake in oven for 30 to 45 minutes (depending on the size).

⁌ Meanwhile, rub the salmon with 1 tablespoon sesame oil, place the salmon in a baking dish, and top with 2 cloves chopped garlic, the juice of one lemon, salt, black pepper and cayenne pepper. Bake in oven with squash for approximately 8 to 12 minutes or until salmon easily flakes with a fork.

⁌ As those are cooking, add 1 tablespoon sesame oil, kale, 1 teaspoon butter (or olive oil), the juice from half of a lemon and 1 clove chopped garlic to medium pan and sauté until kale is slightly wilted. Season with salt and black pepper to taste.

⁌ Remove the squash from the oven, let cool enough to handle. Scrape with a fork (width-wise) to make "spaghetti." Add butter (or olive oil) and combine.

⁌ Place squash on plates, top with kale and then salmon.

LEMON GARLIC CHICKEN

Serves: 4

4 boneless chicken breasts
1 clove garlic, minced
2 teaspoons olive oil
¼ teaspoon cayenne pepper
2 teaspoons lemon juice
3 teaspoons fresh basil
½ teaspoon sea salt

∾ Preheat oven to 350° F.

∾ Combine the garlic, olive oil, cayenne pepper, lemon juice, basil, and salt in a container. Place the chicken breasts in the same container and let marinate for 10 to 15 minutes.

∾ Cover cookie sheet with parchment paper or spray with oil to prevent sticking. Place the chicken breasts on the pan, and bake for approximately 20 to 30 minutes or until done.

Notes:

LOADED BISON BURGER

Serves: 4

1 pound ground bison
½ pound spicy sausage
1 teaspoon sea salt
1 teaspoon black pepper
½ teaspoon minced garlic
Pinch cayenne pepper (optional)

Toppings:
4 cups of spinach
1 cup of sauerkraut
1 avocado, sliced
½ cup shiitake mushrooms, stems removed, sliced

Preheat oven to 350° F.

In a large bowl, mix together bison burger ingredients. Do not over mix. Form into four patties.

Cook patties for approximately 5 minutes on each side or until done to your liking.

Add spinach and sauerkraut to plates.

Then, add bison burger, avocado slices and mushrooms.

Notes:

Your cells are made from the food you eat; healthy food, healthy cells.

Saucy Meatballs *page 144*

Easy 5 Minute Greens and Garbanzo Beans *page 122*

LOADED SWEET POTATO WITH CHICKEN

Serves: 1

1 small sweet potato
2 leaves kale, Swiss chard or spinach, cut into ribbons
1 cup chicken breast strips or shredded chicken
2 tablespoons organic salsa
¼ cup guacamole or ½ avocado

↪ Preheat oven to 375° F

↪ Bake sweet potato for 50 to 60 minutes or until softens.

↪ When there are 10 minutes left on the potato, sauté the greens, chicken and salsa until heated through and the greens have wilted.

↪ When potato is ready, slice in half and top both halves with greens mixture and guacamole or avocado.

Notes:

NUTTY VEGGIE MEDLEY WITH GOAT CHEESE

Serves: 2

1 tablespoon coconut oil
½ medium red onion
½ zucchini, diced
1 cup shiitake mushrooms
2 cloves garlic, minced
4 cups baby spinach
½ cup goat cheese
1 tomato, diced
1 avocado, sliced
½ cup raw walnuts
Sea salt and black pepper to taste

↩ Sauté red onion and zucchini in coconut oil for 5 minutes. Add mushrooms and garlic. Sauté for another 4 minutes (or until mushrooms have softened and onions are translucent). Add baby spinach and heat until spinach begins to wilt.

↩ Remove from heat, add in goat cheese, tomatoes, avocado, and walnuts. Season with salt and pepper.

Notes:

OH, SO SLOPPY JOES

Makes 8 sandwiches

1 tablespoon coconut oil

¼ cup red onion, chopped

¼ cup green pepper, chopped

1 teaspoon garlic, minced

1 pound grass-fed, ground beef

1 cup warm water

2 tablespoons each: onion powder and paprika

1 teaspoon each: garlic powder, chili powder, red pepper flakes, marjoram, dry mustard, sea salt

½ teaspoon black pepper

¼ teaspoon celery seed

¼ teaspoon toasted, ground black cumin seeds (optional)

Pinch cayenne pepper

15-ounce can of diced tomatoes, drained

6-ounce can tomato paste

Ezekiel hamburger buns

In a large skillet, over medium heat, melt the coconut oil. Add onion, green pepper, garlic and cook for 3 to 4 minutes. Add ground beef and cook until meat is browned.

In a bowl mix together warm water and seasoning, stirring until dissolved. Add the diced tomatoes and tomato paste; mix well. Pour over meat mixture and simmer for 5 minutes or until heated through and slightly thickened.

Top the hamburger buns with the mixture and serve.

Notes:

OPEN-FACED EGG SANDWICH

2 slices turkey bacon
1 organic, free-range egg
1 slice Ezekiel bread, toasted
Organic butter
3 avocado slices

Cook turkey bacon in medium pan.

Meanwhile, lightly grease small pan with coconut oil. Add egg and cook over medium heat. Flip partway through cooking.

Toast Ezekiel bread.

Compile open-faced sandwich.

Notes:

PURPLE PUNCH STIR-FRY

Serves: 3-4

1 tablespoon sesame oil
1 tablespoon coconut oil
1 tablespoon garlic, chopped
½ red onion, chopped
1 medium/large green pepper, chopped
1 celery stalk, chopped
½ head purple cauliflower, cut into florets
¼ head of purple cabbage, shredded
¼ cup organic, low-sodium vegetable broth
4 or 5 Swiss chard leaves
¼ cup currants
2 tablespoons raw sesame seeds
¼ teaspoon sea salt
¼ teaspoon black pepper
⅛ to ¼ teaspoon cayenne pepper (optional)

☙ Heat sesame and coconut oil in a large skillet. Add garlic, onion, green pepper, celery, cauliflower and cabbage to the skillet and cook for 6 to 8 minutes.

☙ Add vegetable broth and bring to a low boil.

☙ Add Swiss chard, currants, sesame seeds, salt, black pepper and cayenne pepper to the skillet. Cook until the Swiss chard is slightly wilted. Add more vegetable broth if needed.

Notes:

RISE & SHINE BREAKFAST BURRITO

1 tablespoon coconut or grapeseed oil
1 cup fresh spinach or ½ cup frozen spinach*
¼ cup drained, rinsed canned black beans
Dash sea salt and black pepper
2 organic, free-range eggs
2 tablespoons organic salsa
¼ avocado, diced
BALi-friendly tortilla, optional**

* If using frozen spinach, thaw it in a colander, and then use a towel to squeeze out the excess liquid.

** See recipes to make your own tortillas or buy BALi-friendly tortillas. See Appendix A for resources.

Add oil, spinach, beans, salt and pepper to a medium pan. Sauté over medium-high heat until spinach is slightly wilted and beans are warmed. Transfer to a bowl.

In another bowl, whisk the eggs. Add the eggs to the medium skillet and scramble until cooked through, about 3 minutes.

Spread tortilla with salsa, add black bean/spinach mixture, eggs, then top with avocado. Roll up and serve.

Notes:

ROASTED SWEET POTATOES & CHICKEN

Serves: 4

Marinade ingredients:
5 tablespoons olive oil
3 tablespoons raw honey
1 tablespoon oregano
2 tablespoons garlic, chopped
2 teaspoons sea salt
2 teaspoons paprika
1 teaspoon black pepper

Ingredients:
1 pound chicken, cubed
2 cubed/unpeeled sweet potatoes

✎ Preheat oven to 450° F.

✎ Mix the marinade ingredients well and divide in half.

✎ Add the potatoes and chicken to half the marinade and toss to coat.

✎ Add to a 13 x 9-inch pan and pour remaining marinade over. Roast for 35 minutes.

Recipe contributed by Jessica Sutterfield (RealResultsFitness.net).

Notes:

SALMON CAKES

14.75-ounce can wild salmon, drained
2 organic, free-range eggs, beaten
4 green onions, chopped
¼ cup rolled oats (not instant)
2 garlic cloves, minced
2 tablespoons green onions
2 teaspoons organic Dijon mustard
½ teaspoon paprika
½ teaspoon sea salt
½ teaspoon black pepper
Coconut oil for cooking

Note: You can add more oats if the consistency is runny.

꿀 Combine all of the ingredients in a medium-size bowl.

꿀 Press salmon between your palms to form patties, and set aside.

꿀 In a large pan over medium-high heat, melt enough coconut oil to create a thin layer of oil. Place patties in the pan. Allow the patties to brown on 1 side before flipping and cook all the way through.

꿀 Serve warm or cold as leftovers. These can be paired with a salad and topped with olive oil and balsamic vinegar.

Notes:

SALMON VEGGIE PACKETS

Serves: 4

1½ cups each, thinly sliced: onions, purple carrots, red pepper

1 cup celery, thinly sliced

¼ cup olive oil

Sea salt and black pepper

1½ pounds Alaskan salmon or other fish, separated into 4 portions

1 lemon

Old Bay Seasoning, parsley, sea salt, pepper to taste

Note: You could use any variety of vegetables in these packets based on your preferences.

↩ Preheat oven to 375° F.

↩ Sauté the vegetables in oil until semi-soft, approximately 7 to 9 minutes (based on thickness). Season with salt and pepper.

↩ Cut 4 large pieces of parchment paper to make the packets (seals juices inside). Drizzle each sheet lightly with olive oil.

↩ Fill each packet with a quarter of the cooked veggies. Top with fish, a splash of lemon juice, Old Bay, parsley, salt and pepper.

↩ Fold the packets closed, place on a baking sheet and bake 10 to 15 minutes (the fish should flake easily if it's done).

↩ Carefully open the packets and place the contents on each plate. Pour the sauce from the packet over the top.

Notes:

SAUCY MEATBALLS

Makes approximately 18-20 meatballs

Sauce ingredients:

1 jar of organic marinara sauce

1½ cups of water

Meatball ingredients:

1½ pounds ground, grass-fed beef

1 organic free-range egg

1 tablespoon extra virgin olive oil

½ cup Mary's Gone Crackers Breadcrumbs or Ezekiel breadcrumbs (see recipe)

½ cup red onion, finely chopped

2 teaspoons sea salt

1 teaspoon ground black pepper

½ teaspoon cayenne pepper

1 teaspoon Italian seasoning

½ teaspoon garlic powder

¼ cup freshly shredded Parmesan cheese

In a saucepan, add marinara sauce and water. Cook on low-medium heat.

In a bowl, gently mix all meatball ingredients together. Form meatballs to the size of a golf ball.

Place meatballs in the sauce, cover halfway and slowly simmer for approximately 1 hour or until the meatballs are cooked through.

Notes:

SESAME BAKED SALMON

Serves: 4

4 tablespoons sesame oil

2 lemons, juiced

½ teaspoon ginger powder or 2 tablespoons minced ginger

2 teaspoons chopped garlic

4 salmon fillets

Sea salt and black pepper to taste

↝ Preheat oven to 350° F. Prepare a glass dish or baking sheet with parchment paper or coconut oil.

↝ Combine sesame oil, lemon juice, ginger, and garlic in a small bowl.

↝ Brush the salmon on both sides with the marinade.

↝ Bake the salmon for 20 minutes or until it flakes easily with a fork.

Notes:

SHRIMP SCAMPI

Serves: 4

1 package black bean pasta

2 tablespoons olive oil

2 tablespoons grass-fed, organic butter

1 large shallot, finely chopped

5 cloves fresh garlic, chopped

1 pound shrimp, shelled

1 lemon, juiced

¼ teaspoon lemon zest

Sea salt, black pepper and cayenne pepper to taste

½ cup fresh parsley

Dinner in less than 20 minutes.

❧ Cook pasta according to package directions.

❧ In a medium pan, add olive oil, butter, shallot and garlic. Cook until shallots are translucent and soft.

❧ Add the shrimp, lemon, lemon zest, salt, black pepper and cayenne pepper to pan and cook for approximately 3 to 5 minutes or until pink.

❧ Add chopped parsley and serve over black bean pasta.

Notes:

Shrimp Scampi *page 146*

A healthy relationship with food will have a positive impact on your health.

Salmon Cakes *page 142*

SOUTHWEST RICE & BEANS

1 cup red or black rice
Organic rotisserie chicken
1 tablespoon chili powder
½ teaspoon garlic powder
½ teaspoon onion powder
⅛ teaspoon red pepper flakes
¼ teaspoon dried oregano
½ teaspoon paprika
1½ teaspoons ground cumin
1 teaspoon sea salt
1 teaspoon black pepper
½ cup hot water
1 can black beans, drained and rinsed
1 jar fire-roasted tomatoes

This is a quick and easy dinner. You can use these leftovers as filling in a BALi-friendly tortilla for lunch another day.

❧ Cook rice according to package directions.

❧ While rice is cooking, pull chicken off in pieces and add to another pan.

❧ Add seasoning, water, black beans and tomatoes to pan. Cook until heated through.

❧ Place over cooked rice and serve.

Notes:

SPAGHETTI WITH EASY MARINARA SAUCE

Serves: 3-4

1 tablespoon coconut oil

1 medium red onion

2 green peppers

½ tablespoon of chopped garlic

½ cup of pure pomegranate wine (or red wine)

1 jar of organic spaghetti sauce (no sugar added)

15-ounce container organic diced tomatoes

½ teaspoon sea salt

1 teaspoon black pepper

½ teaspoon crushed red pepper

1 teaspoon basil

1 teaspoon thyme

¾ cup mushrooms

¼ cup green olives (halved)

Organic brown rice spaghetti or any other BALi pasta

Grated Parmesan cheese (optional)

≈ Melt the coconut oil in a medium pot. Add the onion, peppers, and garlic and cook until vegetables are almost soft (approximately 3 to 5 minutes).

≈ Add in the wine, spaghetti sauce, diced tomatoes, salt, black pepper, crushed red pepper, basil and thyme. Bring to a boil, lower heat and simmer for 15 minutes. While the sauce is cooking, make your pasta of choice.

≈ Add in the mushrooms and olives to the tomato sauce and stir to combine.

≈ Place pasta on a plate, top with sauce and grated Parmesan cheese.

Notes:

SPINACH, PEPPERS, & BLACK BEAN OMELET

Serves: 1

2 teaspoons coconut oil
¼ medium red onion, diced
¼ cup bell peppers, diced
1 cup spinach
¼ cup black beans, rinsed, drained
2 organic, free-range eggs
Sea salt and black pepper to taste
½ avocado, sliced

❧ Add oil, onion and peppers to a small pan over medium heat. Sauté for 4 minutes. Add beans and spinach, sautéing until slightly wilted and peppers/onions have softened. Set aside vegetables in a bowl.

❧ In another bowl, scramble eggs, salt and pepper with a fork. Add the eggs to the pan. Cook until the eggs have set.

❧ Flip the eggs over and cook for 3 to 4 minutes. Add the vegetables to one side of the eggs and fold over. Remove from pan, add salt and pepper to taste and top with avocado.

Notes:

STUFFED GRAPE LEAVES

Makes 5 dozen

16-ounce jar grape leaves, rinsed and de-stemmed

2 pounds turkey, pork, lamb, chicken or beef, cooked

1¼ cup red rice

2 tablespoons dried mint

2 tablespoons ground cinnamon

2 tablespoons garlic, minced, divided

1 tablespoon dried parsley

1½ cup lemon juice, divided

¼ cup olive oil

Sea salt and black pepper

1 tomato, sliced

1 large onion, sliced

1 cup water

Paprika

Notes:

Combine meat, rice, mint, cinnamon, 1 tablespoon garlic, parsley, ½ cup lemon juice, olive oil, salt and pepper in a bowl.

Assemble the grape leaves by adding the meat mixture to the grape leaves and rolling. There are videos on You Tube to show you how to do this.

Add the tomato slices and onions to the bottom of a pressure cooker. Then, add a single layer of grape leaf rolls. Add another layer, alternating the pattern. Avoid packing them too tightly in the layers.

Add the remaining 1 tablespoon of minced garlic and 1 cup lemon juice to the pot along with 1 cup of water. Sprinkle paprika on top.

Once the pressure is up, cook for 7 to 12 minutes.

Recipe contributed by J. Kevin Martin, D.C.

STUFFED MEATBALLS

Serves: 4-6

1 block mozzarella cheese

1 container cherry tomatoes or green olives

1 pound grass-fed ground beef or bison

1 pound nitrate-free Italian sausage

½ teaspoon garlic powder

2 teaspoons sea salt

1 teaspoon black pepper

1 cup BALi-approved breadcrumbs (see recipe)

¼ cup freshly shredded Parmesan cheese

2 organic, free-range eggs

½ cup full-fat, unsweetened, organic coconut milk

½ cup chopped parsley

1 jar marinara sauce

Notes:

↩ Cut the mozzarella cheese into ¾-inch cubes. Store in the refrigerator while preparing the meat. You can skip this step if you are using cherry tomatoes or green olives.

↩ In a large mixing bowl, combine the beef/bison, sausage, garlic powder, salt, black pepper, breadcrumbs, Parmesan, eggs, coconut milk and parsley.

↩ Roll golf ball sized balls with the meat mixture. Squish the mozzarella cube, cherry tomato or green olive into the center and pull the edges of the meatball around it until it's a new ball again. Make sure to have enough meat to cover the stuffing.

↩ Arrange the meatballs in a slow cooker and cover in tomato sauce.

↩ Cook on high for 2 to 2.5 hours or low for up to 6 to 8 hours.

Note: You can pan sear the meatballs on all sides on the stovetop first for better flavor and to get rid of some grease. Cook them ½ to ¾ of the way, then transfer them to the slow cooker.

Baking option: You can bake them for about 20 minutes at 400° F (just enough to cook the outside and get rid of the fat).

VEGGIE MEDLEY WITH EGGS & AVOCADO

Serves: 2

2 tablespoons coconut oil
½ cup cauliflower
½ cup broccoli
½ cup green pepper, chopped
½ cup snow peas, chopped
½ cup shiitake mushrooms
½ red onion, chopped
½ cup spinach, chopped
1 cup cherry tomatoes
1 avocado, sliced
2 organic, free-range eggs

✎ Add coconut oil to pan over medium heat. Add cauliflower, broccoli, green peppers, snow peas, mushrooms, and red onion to pan. Sauté for 8 minutes or until vegetables have begun to soften.

✎ Meanwhile, cook eggs over easy in another pan.

✎ Add in spinach to vegetable mixture and sauté for 1 minute. Remove from heat. Stir in cherry tomatoes.

✎ Serve vegetables with eggs and avocado slices.

Notes:

BALi Testimonial

"At 57 years old and menopausal, I have lost 50-plus pounds following the BALi Eating Plan®. In addition, my endurance has increased, I constantly get compliments on my complexion and I no longer suffer from overwhelming anxiety. The recipes in *Simply* BALi are delicious and family-friendly. *Simply* BALi includes real food, sustainable nutrition and can be adopted for any food philosophy or religion. The BALi lifestyle is an enjoyable, easy, and delicious way to live. Start your own transformation. If I can do it, anyone can!"

Robin Martinez, M.D., M.H.A.

PIZZAS & TORTILLAS

BBQ CHICKEN PIZZA

Serves: 2

Pizza crust of choice*
2 cups shredded, cooked chicken
½ cup no-sugar-added barbecue sauce
½ red bell pepper, diced
2 scallions, diced
Handful spinach, chopped
¾ cup cheese (optional)

* See Appendix A for Resources.

Preheat oven to 400° F.

Put the pizza crust on a pizza stone or cookie sheet.

Combine the chicken and barbecue sauce in a medium bowl.

Layer each pizza with chicken, peppers, scallions, spinach, and optional cheese.

Bake for 15 minutes or until done.

Note: To quickly cook chicken to use in this pizza, you can place 2 to 3 chicken breasts (enough for 2 cups chicken) in a medium saucepan. Add lightly salted water to cover chicken and bring to a boil. Cover, reduce heat and simmer gently until the chicken is cooked through and no longer pink in the middle, 10 to 15 minutes. You can even do this ahead of time, so it is ready to use.

Notes:

COCONUT PIZZA CRUST

Makes 1 small crust

¼ cup plus 2 tablespoons coconut flour
¼ cup coconut oil
3 organic, free-range eggs
1 teaspoon raw honey
1 teaspoon aluminum-free baking powder
¼ teaspoon sea salt

❧ Preheat oven to 350° F. Line a pizza sheet with parchment paper.

❧ Mix together the wet ingredients in one bowl and the dry ingredients in another. Combine the wet and dry ingredients

❧ Roll batter onto parchment paper until about ½ to ¾ -inch thick.

❧ Bake for 20 minutes. Take the crust out and top with favorite ingredients.

❧ Place back in oven to bake for another 2 to 3 minutes or just until the cheese has melted.

Notes:

CREATE YOUR OWN PIZZA

> Makes 1 pizza

There are many ways you can make a pizza. Think about the toppings you like best and create your own. Be creative and try many different toppings.

Crusts:

Cauliflower crust
Eggplant
Ezekiel tortillas
Grain-free pizza crust
Guiltless pizza crust*
Zucchini

Pizza Sauces:

Barbecue sauce
Olive oil
Pesto
Tomato sauce

Meat Toppings:

Bacon, nitrate-free
Chicken
Chili
Ground beef, grass-fed
Ham
Meatballs
Pepperoni, nitrate free
Pork, shredded
Sausage
Steak strips, grass-fed

Vegetable Toppings:

Artichokes
Basil
Broccoli
Cilantro
Eggplant
Garlic
Green bell peppers
Mixed, grilled vegetables
Mushrooms
Olives
Red bell peppers
Red onion
Roasted red peppers
Spinach
Tomatoes

Cheese Toppings:

Cheddar cheese
Feta cheese
Goat cheese
Mozzarella cheese
Parmesan cheese

Leftovers:

Really this can be anything (chili, salad, etc.)

* See Appendix A for Resources.

EGGPLANT PIZZAS

Serves: 4

Sea salt (enough to season eggplant)
1 eggplant, sliced
¼ cup extra virgin olive oil
3 tablespoons garlic, chopped
2 teaspoons Italian seasoning
Sea salt and black pepper
1 cup feta cheese
1 avocado, sliced
1 tomato, sliced
2 tablespoons Parmesan cheese
Optional: Banana peppers for serving

❧ Salt the eggplant slices and let sit for 15 minutes to bring the moisture out. Then, pat down with a paper towel.

❧ Preheat oven to 400° F. Line baking sheet with parchment paper.

❧ Add eggplant slices to the baking sheet and then top with olive oil, garlic, Italian seasoning, salt, pepper, feta cheese, avocado, tomato, and Parmesan cheese.

❧ Bake for 15 minutes or until cooked through and cheese has melted.

Notes:

HOMEMADE TORTILLAS

Makes 8-12 tortillas

- 4 organic, free-range eggs
- 2 tablespoons coconut oil, gently melted
- 2 tablespoons or more water
- ½ cup arrowroot powder
- 2 tablespoons coconut flour
- 2 tablespoons any other flour (spelt, almond, etc.)
- ½ teaspoon sea salt
- 2 tablespoons grass-fed, organic butter or ghee

These can be used as crepes, wraps or sandwiches.

Combine the eggs, coconut oil, and water in a small bowl.

Combine the arrowroot, coconut flour, other flour and salt in a medium bowl.

Gradually add the liquid mixture, stirring constantly.

Add about ⅛ cup onto a hot, buttered skillet. Sprinkle some salt on each. Cook 1 minute on each side or until bubbles form. Cook until lightly browned.

Notes:

MEATY PIZZA

Pizza crust of choice*
½ cup pizza sauce
¼ cup packed baby spinach, cut into ribbons
¼ cup nitrate-free sliced pepperoni
¼ cup nitrate-free Italian sausage
1 cup cheese (optional)
1 teaspoon Italian seasoning
Sea salt and black pepper

* See Appendix A for Resources.

ᴥ Preheat oven to 425° F.

ᴥ In a medium pan, cook the sausage.

ᴥ Spoon the pizza sauce over the pizza crust. Top with baby spinach, pepperoni, sausage, optional cheese and pepper.

ᴥ Bake for 10 to 20 minutes or until desired crispness is reached.

Notes:

MEDITERRANEAN CHICKEN & HUMMUS PIZZA

Serves: 2-4

Pizza crust of choice*
1 cup hummus
½ pound shredded chicken
¼ teaspoon dried rosemary
1 cup spinach, cut into ribbons
¾ cup goat cheese

* See Appendix A for Resources.

∾ Preheat oven to 400° F.

∾ Spread hummus evenly over pizza crust. Combine chicken and rosemary in a medium bowl, and then add it to the pizza.

∾ Top with spinach and goat cheese.

∾ Bake for 8 to 12 minutes (or until cheese softens and the pizza is hot). Let stand for 5 minutes and cut into slices.

Notes:

MEXICAN PIZZA

Serves: 4

4 BALi-friendly tortillas*
1 can refried beans
Handful spinach
1 can black beans, drained, rinsed
2 cups medium organic salsa
½ cup green onions, chopped
1 cup Mexican cheese (optional)

Note: For more spice, use hot salsa. It has a very thin crust, so it may be easier to eat with a knife/fork.

* See recipes to make your own tortillas, choose BALi-friendly tortillas or see Appendix A for resources.

🍃 Preheat oven to broiler high heat.

🍃 With the rack in the middle of the oven, place the tortillas on the rack and toast for 2 minutes (watch to make sure they don't burn). Then, flip and toast again for 2 minutes. You want them to be toasted and slightly crisp, but not too crisp because they will be going back in the oven.

🍃 Place the tortillas onto 2 cookie sheets. Spread ¼ cup of the refried beans on each tortilla, and then top with spinach, black beans, tomatoes, salsa, green onions and optional cheese. Place the pizzas back under the broiler, and bake for 3 to 4 minutes just to warm the toppings. Remove and cut into pizza slices with a pizza cutter.

Notes:

SPELT CREPES OR TORTILLAS

Makes 10 - 12 crepes or tortillas

3 cups spelt flour
½ teaspoon aluminum-free baking powder
¾ teaspoon sea salt
1 cup hot water
4 tablespoons coconut oil

In a medium bowl, combine the flour, baking powder, and salt.

In a measuring cup, mix hot water and oil.

Slowly add to flour mixture and stir with a fork. Knead dough until smooth (10 to 15 strokes). Divide into 10 to 12 balls. Cover with a damp towel and let sit for 30 minutes.

Roll out and cook for 1 minute, then flip and cook for 1 more minute.

Recipe by Eixor Johnson

Notes:

Healthy isn't a goal, it's a way of living.

Create Your Own Pizza *page 159*

BBQ Chicken Pizza *page 157*

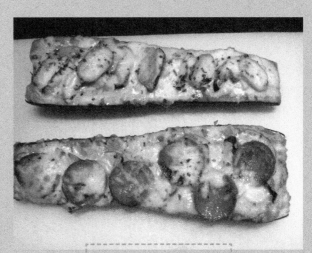

Zucchini Pizzas *page 168*

VEGGIE PIZZA

Serves: 1

Pizza crust of choice or 2 BALi-friendly
tortillas*

1 tablespoon extra virgin olive oil

½ cup tomato sauce

2 tablespoons mozzarella cheese

Sea salt, black pepper and cayenne pepper

1 tablespoon Italian seasoning

2 tablespoons Parmesan cheese

1½ cup vegetables (broccoli, tomatoes, red
onion, etc.)

½ cup shredded cheddar cheese

* See Appendix A for Resources.

≈ Preheat oven to 425° F.

≈ Brush 1 tortilla with olive oil, and then sprinkle with mozzarella cheese. Place another tortilla on top of that (so they melt together and make the crust thicker). Brush the top tortilla with olive oil. Then, top with remaining ingredients.

≈ Bake for 12 minutes or until cooked through and cheese is melted.

Notes: _____

_____

_____

_____

ZUCCHINI PIZZAS

1 zucchini
Extra virgin olive oil
½ cup tomato sauce
1 large steak tomato, sliced
½ cup shredded cheddar cheese
¼ cup shredded Parmesan cheese
Dulse flakes
Sea salt, black pepper and cayenne pepper to taste

Takes only 15 minutes. Quick and easy!

↩ Preheat oven to 375° F.

↩ Slice zucchini lengthwise and in half. Brush with olive oil.

↩ Spoon the sauce over the zucchini.

↩ Top with tomatoes, cheddar cheese, Parmesan cheese, salt, dulse flakes, black pepper and cayenne pepper to taste.

↩ Bake zucchini for 6 minutes, then add tomatoes and bake for another 6 minutes (or until cheese has melted). Serve.

Notes:

SOUPS & STEWS

BEEF STEW

Serves: 4

1 pound stewing beef
2 tablespoons coconut oil
4 cups beef broth
1 cup red onion, chopped
1 cup celery, chopped
3 purple carrots, chopped
2 sweet potatoes, cubed
28-ounce can diced tomatoes
¼ teaspoon dried rosemary
¼ teaspoon dried thyme
Sea salt and black pepper to taste
2 cups Swiss chard, cut into ribbons

In a large saucepan over medium-high heat, combine the onions, celery, carrots, sweet potatoes and coconut oil. Cook for 3 to 5 minutes, stirring constantly.

Add the beef, tomatoes, broth, rosemary and thyme. Season to taste with salt and pepper.

Cover the saucepan and cook for about 1 hour, allowing the stew to simmer. Stir a few times during the cooking process.

Remove the lid, add Swiss chard and cook uncovered for about 45 minutes. If the mixture is too thick at the end of the cooking process, you can add a little bit of water or stock.

Notes:

CHICKEN & RICE SOUP

8 cups chicken broth, divided

1 medium onion, diced

3 medium purple carrots, diced

2 stalks celery, diced

2 cups water

1 cup black rice

1 medium chicken breast, cut into ½-inch cubes

3 cups frozen chopped kale or spinach or 1 whole bunch fresh kale (chopped)

1 whole bay leaf

1 teaspoon black pepper

1 to 2 teaspoons sea salt, to taste

Optional: 1 tablespoon lemon juice to taste

Vegetarian option: replace chicken with shiitake mushrooms.

In a large pot over medium-high heat, add ½ cup broth, onion, carrots and celery and simmer for 8 minutes, stirring occasionally.

Add remaining 7 ½ cups broth, water, rice, chicken, bay leaf, pepper and salt and bring to a boil. Reduce heat to medium, cover and cook for 35 minutes (or until rice is tender and chicken cooked through).

Remove bay leaf and stir in kale or spinach. Continue cooking until the kale is wilted and tender, about 3 to 5 minutes.

Notes:

CHICKEN TORTILLA SOUP

Serves: 6-7

2 large chicken breasts
28-ounce container diced tomatoes*
32 ounces chicken broth
1 to 2 cups water
1 medium red onion, diced
1 jalapeno, seeded and diced
2 cups shredded carrots
2 cups celery, diced
2 cloves minced garlic
2 tablespoons tomato paste
1 teaspoon sea salt
1 teaspoon chili powder
1 teaspoon cumin
2 tablespoons lime juice

Optional toppings:
~ Avocado
~ Black beans
~ Cilantro

You can use fire-roasted tomatoes.

Notes:

~ Place all ingredients (including black beans if adding) in a crock-pot and cook on high 4 to 6 hours or low 8 to 10 hours.

~ Remove chicken once cooked thoroughly, shred with two forks. Return to the crock-pot, mix in and your soup is ready! Serve with optional toppings.

Serve with:
~ Beanitos
~ Spelt chips

CREAMY BROCCOLI SOUP

1 medium onion, roughly chopped

1 tablespoon coconut oil or olive oil

$\frac{1}{8}$ teaspoon ground nutmeg

4 cups chicken broth, reduced sodium

1$\frac{1}{2}$ cups water

$\frac{1}{3}$ cup rolled oats (not instant)

1$\frac{1}{2}$ pounds broccoli, florets separated, cut into $\frac{1}{2}$-inch rounds*

Sea salt and black pepper to taste

*Note: You can substitute frozen broccoli florets for the fresh broccoli. Just decrease the water to 1 cup.

꧁ In a large saucepan, heat oil over medium heat. Add onion and cook until softened, about 5 minutes, stirring occasionally.

꧁ Add nutmeg and cook for another 30 seconds.

꧁ Stir in broth, 1$\frac{1}{2}$ cups water, oats and broccoli. Season with salt and pepper. Bring to a boil, and reduce heat. Simmer until broccoli is tender, 5 to 10 minutes.

꧁ Puree soup in batches, filling blender halfway. Return to pot. Season with salt and pepper.

Blender Tip: Hot liquids tend to expand when blended, so be careful not to fill the blender more than halfway each time.

Notes:

Chicken Tortilla Soup *page 173*

"Soup is a lot like family. Each ingredient enhances the others; each batch has its own characteristics; and it needs time to simmer to reach full flavor."

- Marge Kennedy

Tailgate Chilli *page 182*

Lentils & Vegetable Bowl *page 180*

CRITTERS BE GONE GARLIC SOUP

Serves: 6

30 garlic cloves (can use jarred organic peeled garlic)

2 tablespoons avocado oil

3 tablespoons ghee or grass-fed, organic butter

1 teaspoon cayenne powder

1 teaspoon turmeric

¾ cup ginger (finely chopped or grated)

2 cups purple onions (sliced)

2 teaspoons fresh thyme (chopped)

⅛ teaspoon sea salt

½ teaspoon black pepper

30 garlic cloves (can use jarred organic peeled garlic)

1 cup full-fat, unsweetened, organic coconut milk

4 cups bone broth or low-sodium organic vegetable broth

≈ Layer the first 30 garlic cloves in Corningware dish with lid. Coat the garlic cloves with the avocado oil and sprinkle with salt. Cover baking dish and bake until garlic is tender, about 30 to 45 minutes. Transfer cloves to small bowl.

≈ Melt ghee or butter in a pan over medium heat. Add cayenne powder, turmeric, ginger, onions, thyme, salt, and pepper, cook for about 6 to 10 minutes. Add the roasted garlic and 30 raw garlic cloves and cook for another 5 minutes. Add vegetable broth, cover and simmer for 20 to 30 minutes. Add small batches to a high-speed blender and puree. On slow speed add in the coconut milk. Return to the pan and heat until hot but not boiling.

Notes:

EASY CROCK-POT ROAST CHICKEN BONE BROTH

Varies based on crock-pot size

Bones, skin and seasonings from Easy Crock-pot Roast Chicken recipe

Filtered water

1 tablespoon apple cider vinegar

❧ Make the Easy Crock-pot Roast Chicken recipe. Remove the meat from the bones. Add the bones and the skin back into the crock-pot.

❧ Add filtered water to just cover the chicken bones and pieces. Add the apple cider vinegar.

❧ Cover the crock-pot and simmer on low for 12 to 36 hours.

❧ Carefully strain the broth through a fine metal sieve and discard the bones.

Notes:

Storage of Broth

After your stock is cooked, put what you want to use right away in the refrigerator. It will keep for about a week. The broth will likely gelatinize in your refrigerator overnight. You want this gelatin because it's very good for your digestion, plus it helps support the connective tissues in your body.

Freeze the remaining broth in Mason jars. Make sure to allow for expansion in the jars (only fill about ¾ of the way full). You can even freeze some of it for future use in ice cube trays for quick defrosting.

I've got bone broth – What do I do with it now?

Bone broth can be very simply consumed by sipping from a mug like tea, along with your dinner. Some people prefer to drink it in the mornings instead of coffee. For therapeutic benefits, do this one to three times per day. Beyond that, use your broth as the base for soups/sauces and to cook rice/quinoa (or in any recipe that calls for stock).

Notes:

KALE & BROCCOLI SOUP

Serves: 4

1 small head of broccoli, chopped
½ bunch of kale, chopped
2 celery stalks, chopped
1 red onion, chopped
1½ cups water
3 cloves garlic, diced
1 tablespoon coconut oil
1½ cups full-fat, unsweetened, organic coconut milk
1½ cup chicken or vegetable bone broth (can use organic, low sodium chicken or vegetable broth)
⅛ teaspoon cayenne pepper
½ teaspoon sea salt
¼ teaspoon black pepper
Hemp seeds (optional)

❧ In blender, mix water and half of the broccoli, kale, celery and red onion.

❧ Add to a large pot and bring to a boil. Lower to simmer, add the rest of the ingredients (except the remaining kale) and simmer for 30 minutes.

❧ Add the kale the last 5 minutes.

❧ For a creamy soup, place everything back into the blender and blend until smooth. If you enjoy the vegetables whole, then skip this step.

❧ Top with hemp seeds (optional) and serve.

Notes:

LENTILS & VEGETABLES BOWL

Serves: 4-6

1 tablespoon coconut oil

1 medium onion, chopped

2 cloves garlic, diced

2 medium carrots, chopped (purple carrots preferred)

2 cups shredded cabbage

2 stalks celery, chopped

1 cup red or green lentils

32-ounce container low sodium vegetable broth

2 teaspoons cumin

3 cups packed fresh kale or 1 cup frozen kale

1 teaspoon sea salt

2 green onions, chopped for garnish

ﾟ Add oil, onions, garlic, carrots, cabbage and celery to a large pot over medium-high heat, sautéing for 10 minutes.

ﾟ Add washed lentils, broth and cumin to the vegetable mixture. Bring to a boil.

ﾟ Lower the heat to medium and simmer covered for 20 minutes.

ﾟ Add kale and salt, simmering for another 2 to 3 minutes, until greens are wilted (or thawed). Serve garnished with scallions.

Notes:

180

OVER-THE-TOP BONE BROTH

Varies based on crock-pot size

Organic beef shoulder
Organic chicken carcass
1 large red onion
1 whole leek
3 celery stalks
1 small horseradish root
5 cloves garlic
1 jalapeno pepper
¼ cup apple cider vinegar
½ teaspoon sea salt
½ teaspoon black pepper
½ teaspoon thyme
Filtered water (enough to cover the ingredients)

Second batch:
1 red onion, sliced
3 cloves garlic
¼ cup apple cider vinegar
Filtered water (enough to cover the ingredients)

Notes:

_____

_____

_____

Remove green portion of the leek.

Chop and add all ingredients to the crock-pot. Add enough water to cover the ingredients.

Cover and cook for 36 hours on low heat.

Strain the liquid from the ingredients with a fine mesh strainer.

Add the ingredients back to the crock-pot. Add the additional ingredients for the second batch. Add enough water to cover the ingredients.

Cover and cook for 24 hours. Strain the liquid from the ingredients with a fine mesh strainer.

Mix the 2 batches together to use and store for future use.

TAILGATE CHILI

Serves: 6

1 red onion, diced

3 cloves garlic, minced

2 pounds ground beef or turkey

1 each: red pepper and green bell pepper, both diced

1 cup zucchini, finely diced

1 jalapeno, minced

2, 28-ounce cans/jars diced tomatoes

29-ounce can black, pinto or kidney beans

3 tablespoons chili powder

1 tablespoon each: oregano, basil

2 teaspoons cumin

1 teaspoon each: sea salt and black pepper

½ teaspoon cayenne (optional)

2 avocados (sliced) for garnish

✍ Sauté onions and garlic together in a large saucepan over medium heat. Add in ground beef (or turkey) to the saucepan and cook just until browned.

✍ Add all of the remaining ingredients (except avocado) to the saucepan.

✍ Cook for an additional 30 minutes or until the vegetables have cooked and the flavors have combined well.

✍ Spoon into individual bowls. Garnish with avocado.

Notes:

SIDES

BAKED PARSNIP FRIES

Serves: 4

4 parsnips, peeled and cut into fries
¼ cup parsley, finely chopped
¼ cup olive oil
1 tablespoon sea salt
1 teaspoon black pepper

❧ Preheat oven to 450° F.

❧ Toss all the ingredients together in a large bowl and spread the fries onto a baking tray.

❧ Bake for 40 minutes.

Notes:

BRUSSELS SPROUTS WITH BACON

4 slices bacon, chopped
1 small shallot, diced
1 tablespoon apple cider vinegar
1 pound Brussels sprouts, stemmed and halved
1 tablespoon olive oil

❧ Heat skillet over medium-high heat. Add bacon and shallot to a skillet.

❧ Add olive oil and sprouts to the pan. Cook for about 5 minutes or until sprouts are done to your preference, tossing occasionally.

❧ Pour apple cider vinegar over the sprouts, toss a few more times, and serve immediately.

Notes:

CAULIFLOWER RICE

Serves: 2-4

1 head cauliflower, cut into 1-inch pieces
1 to 3 tablespoons olive oil or ghee, to taste
½ teaspoon sea salt
Black pepper to taste

Note: You can make it with the ingredients listed above, or you can add in anything else you would like. Potential additions are garlic, onion and celery for some variety.

If you have a steamer basket, bring water to a boil. Add in the cauliflower and steam covered for 5 minutes. If you do not have a steamer basket, place water in a pot (enough to cover the cauliflower once it is added), and bring to a boil. Add cauliflower and boil for 5 minutes.

Drain and rinse with cold water to stop the cooking process.

Place cauliflower in food processor and process until the consistency of cooked rice. Do not over process or puree.

Transfer back to cooking pot to reheat, adding in olive oil or ghee, salt and pepper.

Notes:

COLESLAW

1 bag coleslaw

1 bag broccoli slaw

½ cup raw honey

½ cup raw apple cider vinegar

⅓ cup olive oil

½ teaspoon each: sea salt, dry mustard, celery seed, garlic powder, black pepper

🍃 Place a medium saucepan over medium heat and add dressing ingredients to the pan. Stir to combine and bring to a boil.

🍃 Simmer for 3 minutes, stirring occasionally.

🍃 Pour the dressing over the coleslaw mix and toss to coat. Cover and place in the refrigerator for at least 1 hour or until chilled. Taste and adjust any seasonings as needed.

Notes:

GARLIC ZUCCHINI SAUTÉ

Serves: 4

3 tablespoons olive oil

2 pounds squash or zucchini, chopped into pieces

5 cloves of garlic, crushed

~ Heat olive oil in a skillet on medium heat.

~ Add the squash/zucchini to the skillet. Sauté until softened, approximately 10 minutes.

~ Add the garlic and sauté for 1 to 2 more minutes.

Notes:

"Eat food,
not too much,
mostly plants."
- Michael Pollan

Green Bean Almondine *page 191*

Roasted Asparagus with Lemon Vinaigrette *page 193*

Zucchini "Pasta" *page 202*

GREEN BEAN ALMONDINE

Serves: 4

1 pound string beans, ends snapped off
4 to 6 garlic cloves, peeled and whole
2 tablespoons olive oil, coconut oil or ghee
2 teaspoons lemon juice
½ cup slivered almonds
Sea salt to taste

❧ Preheat oven to 425° F.

❧ In a baking dish, add beans, garlic, a pinch of salt, and oil.

❧ Place dish in the oven. Roast until beans are cooked through, about 15 to 20 minutes, stirring halfway through.

❧ Remove from the oven. Toss with the lemon juice and almonds and transfer to a serving dish.

❧ Sprinkle with additional salt.

Notes:

RED QUINOA

1 cup red quinoa
1¼ cup water
1 tablespoon coconut oil
1 tablespoon ghee
Sea salt and black pepper to taste

↝ Prepare quinoa according to package directions.

↝ Once cooked, add in coconut oil, ghee, salt, and pepper. Serve with greens or a green veggie juice.

Notes:

ROASTED ASPARAGUS WITH LEMON VINAIGRETTE

Serves: 3-4

1 bunch fresh asparagus
2 tablespoons olive oil
Sea salt and black pepper, to taste

Optional Lemon Vinaigrette Dressing:
2 tablespoons white wine vinegar
1 tablespoon organic Dijon mustard
1 tablespoon lemon juice
¼ cup olive oil

∾ Preheat oven to 375° F.

∾ Place asparagus on parchment-lined cookie sheet. Drizzle asparagus with olive oil, then sprinkle with salt and pepper. Roast for about 7 to 9 minutes (should still be firm).

∾ Meanwhile, in a small bowl, whisk vinegar, mustard, lemon juice and olive oil.

∾ Transfer asparagus to serving dish and top with optional vinaigrette. Season to taste with salt and pepper.

Notes:
_____
_____
_____

ROASTED BROCCOLI

2 heads broccoli (chopped)
1 tablespoon olive oil
Sea salt and black pepper (to taste)
Juice of ½ lemon

❧ Preheat oven to 450° F.

❧ On a cookie sheet lined with parchment paper, toss the broccoli with the oil, salt and pepper. Spread evenly in a single layer.

❧ Roast until the broccoli has browned in some areas. Squeeze the lemon juice over the broccoli and serve.

Notes:

ROASTED BRUSSELS SPROUTS

Serves: 2-4

4 tablespoons grass-fed, organic butter
2 cloves garlic
½ cup full-fat, unsweetened, organic coconut milk
¼ cup sherry
1 pound Brussels sprouts, halved
Sea salt and black pepper

～ Preheat oven to 475° F.

～ Add the butter, garlic, coconut milk and sherry to a medium pan.

～ Bring to a low boil and add Brussels sprouts. Coat them well and then transfer to a cookie sheet. Top with salt and pepper. Bake for 15 minutes, stirring halfway through.

Notes:

ROASTED VEGGIES

1 tablespoon coconut oil
¼ cup broccoli, chopped
¼ cup red pepper, chopped
¼ medium red onion, diced
¼ cup tomatoes, diced
¼ cup black beans
Pinch of sprouts

~ Add oil, broccoli, peppers, and onions to a small pan over medium heat. Sauté for 4 minutes, then add tomatoes and black beans. Sauté for approximately 4 minutes, or until vegetables are desired tenderness.

~ Put vegetable medley on plate and top with sprouts.

Notes:

Spinach Spaghetti Squash *page 199*

Food is fuel...
Eat to live.

Red Quinoa *page 192*

SIMPLE SPAGHETTI SQUASH

1 large spaghetti squash
Drizzle of olive oil
Dash sea salt and black pepper

Spaghetti squash is a GREAT substitute for pasta. This squash is so easy… just slice, bake and shred. Serving with a jar of marinara sauce can make dinner even easier.

ℰ Preheat oven to 400° F.

ℰ Cut the spaghetti squash length-wise. Be careful, this takes muscle!

ℰ Scrape out the seeds and pulp, as you would with any squash or pumpkin.

ℰ Drizzle cut side with olive oil, salt and pepper.

ℰ Bake on parchment-lined baking sheet, cut side down, about 40 to 60 minutes. When squash is pierced with a fork and appears tender, it is ready.

ℰ Remove from the oven and let it cool slightly. Take a fork and run it along the inside of the squash from end to end. This will separate the strands, so it resembles spaghetti.

Chef Tip: Decrease baking time for smaller spaghetti squash.

Notes:

SPINACH SPAGHETTI SQUASH

Serves: 2-3

1 tablespoon olive oil
6 cloves of garlic, minced
1 large tomato or 2 plum tomatoes, diced
4 cups baby spinach
2 cups cooked spaghetti squash
Sea salt and black pepper to taste

Optional: Parsley for garnish to make it pretty!

↝ In a large skillet, heat the oil over medium heat. Add garlic and cook until just turning brown.

↝ Add the tomatoes, a pinch of salt and spinach. Cover and cook for 2 minutes.

↝ Break up the spinach with a wooden spoon (it will start to clump together once cooked).

↝ Stir in the spaghetti squash a little at a time. Sprinkle with salt and pepper. Once heated through, serve.

Notes:
_____
_____
_____

SWEET POTATO ROUNDS

3 tablespoons coconut oil

1 sweet potato, sliced

Sea salt, cayenne pepper and black pepper to taste

¼ cup plain Greek yogurt

2 tablespoons ground flaxseed

❧ Melt coconut oil in a pan over medium heat. Add sweet potato to pan and cook for 3 to 4 minutes. Turn over, cooking until done and slightly crispy.

❧ Remove potatoes from pan and place on a plate. Top with salt, cayenne pepper, black pepper, Greek yogurt and ground flaxseed.

Notes:

200

SWEET POTATOES WITH ROASTED WALNUTS

Serves: 3-4

1 tablespoon grass-fed, organic butter

1 cup raw walnuts

Pinch sea salt

Pinch cinnamon

Pinch cayenne pepper

2 tablespoons coconut oil

2 sweet potatoes, sliced into medallions or strips

In a medium pan, combine butter, walnuts, salt, and cayenne pepper over low heat. Stir constantly for approximately 3 to 4 minutes. Place in a bowl and set aside.

Heat coconut oil, add sweet potato slices, sprinkle with salt and cook over medium heat for 3 to 4 minutes. Turn the sweet potatoes and cook for another 3 to 4 minutes. Transfer from the pan onto paper towels to absorb the oils. Place the sweet potatoes on plates, top with walnuts and serve.

Notes:

ZUCCHINI "PASTA"

2 to 3 medium zucchini
2 tablespoons olive oil
2 garlic cloves, minced
2 teaspoons lemon zest
½ teaspoon red pepper flakes (optional)
½ pound cherry tomatoes, halved or quartered
Juice from ½ lemon
Fresh basil leaves
Sea salt and black pepper to taste

❧ Using a spiralizer, make noodles out of the zucchini.

❧ In a medium skillet, sauté olive oil, garlic, lemon zest, and optional red pepper flakes for 1 minute.

❧ Add remaining ingredients and sauté for another minute. Serve immediately.

Notes:

SALADS

BASIC MASON JAR SALAD

Serves: 1

Add in your dressing of choice

Choose a grain, protein or heavy ingredients that hold up well when submerged In dressing (beans, cucumbers, broccoli slaw, radishes, red onion)

Leafy greens (spinach, kale, chard)

Accent items (nuts, seeds, cheese)

Mason jar salads are perfect to make ahead and take with you to work or be able to grab them when you are busy. The secret to making the perfect Mason jar salad relies on the order of ingredients. In addition, make sure you use wide mouth Mason jars, so you can get the ingredients out!

If you prepare your Mason jar in this order, you will get a beautiful salad bed when turning over the Mason jar onto a plate.

Notes:

CHOPPED SALAD

¼ cup olive oil

3 tablespoons stone-ground mustard

¼-inch knob ginger

4 cups chopped vegetables: purple cabbage, purple cauliflower, broccoli, Brussels sprouts, zucchini, green pepper, and/or cucumber

¼ cup red onion, diced

1 jalapeno pepper, diced

2 stalks celery, diced

3 tablespoons fresh cilantro, chopped

3 tablespoons pumpkin seeds

2 tablespoons currants

4 boiled organic, free-range eggs, chopped

1 tomato, chopped

1 tablespoon ground flaxseed

Sea salt and black pepper to taste

↬ Combine the olive oil, mustard and ginger in a large bowl.

↬ Add the remaining ingredients to the bowl and toss to combine. Enjoy immediately or put in the refrigerator to allow the flavors to combine.

Notes:

CREAMY CHICKEN SALAD

Serves: 4

1 pound chicken

2 tablespoons Vegenaise

1 teaspoon each: lemon juice, white wine vinegar, organic Dijon mustard, raw honey

⅛ teaspoon each: sea salt and black pepper

1 stalk celery, chopped

½ diced green apple

3 tablespoons raw almonds, chopped

6 cups mixed salad greens

To poach chicken: fill a pot ⅔ full of water and bring to a boil. Add the chicken to the boiling water. Cover and simmer for 20 minutes or until a thermometer registers 165° F. Remove from pan and let stand for 5 minutes. Shred chicken and refrigerate 30 minutes until cold.

Combine Vegenaise, lemon juice, vinegar, Dijon mustard, honey, salt and pepper in a large bowl, stirring with a whisk until combined. Add chicken, celery, apple and almonds. Toss well.

Cover and refrigerate for 1 hour. Serve over salad greens.

Notes:

EGG SALAD

4 hard boiled organic, free-range eggs, diced
1 avocado, diced
½ cup sauerkraut
¼ red onion, diced
¼ cup Vegenaise
1 tablespoon stone-ground mustard
Cayenne pepper to taste
Swiss chard leaves

Combine all ingredients and serve on Swiss chard leaves.

Notes:

GARBANZO BEAN & BROCCOLI SALAD

Serves: 3-4

4 cups broccoli florets
15-ounce can garbanzo beans, drained
5 scallions, diced
½ cup fresh parsley, chopped
⅓ cup pine nuts
1 clove garlic, minced
2 teaspoons organic Dijon mustard
1 teaspoon raw honey
¼ cup lemon juice
6 tablespoons extra-virgin olive oil
Sea salt and black pepper to taste

Steam 4 cups broccoli florets until tender, approximately 5 to 7 minutes.

Meanwhile, add pine nuts to small pan and heat dry over medium heat for approximately 2 to 4 minutes, stirring constantly.

When broccoli is done steaming, rinse with cold water to cool, then chop and combine with garbanzo beans, scallions, parsley, and pine nuts.

To make the dressing, combine garlic, mustard, honey, lemon juice and olive oil in a small bowl, whisking to combine. Season with salt and pepper.

Mix dressing in with broccoli mixture and enjoy!

Note: This can be refrigerated up to 2 days in an airtight container.

Notes:

Every time you eat is an opportunity to nourish your body.

Kale Pomegranate Salad *page 213*

Quick Quinoa Mason Jar Salad *page 217*

Garbanzo Bean & Broccoli Salad *page 209*

KALE & QUINOA SALAD

Serves: 4-6

1 small butternut squash, cubed or 1 container pre-cut butternut squash

1 tablespoon raw honey

½ tablespoon olive oil

Pinch paprika

1 cup red quinoa, uncooked

1 cup water

2 bunches kale, thick stems removed, cut into ribbons

½ cup crumbled goat cheese

½ cup raw walnuts, toasted

1 pomegranate, seeded

1 yellow bell pepper, seeded and diced (optional)

Sea salt and black pepper to taste

Notes:

∾ Preheat oven to 375° F.

∾ Combine squash, honey, olive oil, and paprika. Spread squash onto a parchment paper-lined baking sheet and bake 30 to 45 minutes or until roasted and softened. Stir every 15 minutes. Remove squash from the oven and allow to cool.

∾ Follow the instructions on your quinoa package to cook.

∾ In a large pan, add 1 cup water and kale. Cover and cook on medium-high to steam the kale for 7 to 10 minutes. Remove kale from heat and allow to cool.

∾ Once squash, quinoa, and kale are cooked and cooled to room temperature, combine in a large bowl. Add goat cheese, walnuts, and pomegranate seeds. Toss to combine. Add salt, pepper and additional olive oil as needed.

KALE BLUEBERRY SALAD

¼ cup extra virgin olive oil

¼ cup apple cider vinegar

¼ cup tart cherry juice

4 cups kale, chopped

1 cup garbanzo beans

1 cup cabbage, chopped

1 cup carrots, chopped or shredded

½ red onion, diced

1 cup grape tomatoes

3 tablespoons goji berries

Sea salt, black pepper, cayenne pepper and garlic to taste

1 cup blueberries

½ cup raw cashews

¼ cup raw sunflower seeds

ᴥ Combine the olive oil, apple cider vinegar and tart cherry juice in a large bowl.

ᴥ Add the kale, beans, cabbage, carrots, onion, tomatoes, goji berries, salt, black pepper, cayenne pepper and garlic to the large bowl. Combine well.

ᴥ Add the blueberries, cashews and sunflower seeds and gently combine. Serve immediately or place in the refrigerator and allow the flavors to combine.

Notes:

KALE POMEGRANATE SALAD

Serves: 6

Salad Ingredients:

1 bunch kale, washed, tough stems removed and sliced very thinly

¼ small head red cabbage

1 cup toasted walnuts

½ pomegranate, seeded

2 medium purple carrots, peeled and grated

Dash sea salt

Dressing Ingredients:

½ diced apple

1½ tablespoons apple cider vinegar

2 teaspoons raw honey

2 small cloves garlic

1 teaspoon curry or turmeric powder

¼ cup olive oil

This salad holds up well in the refrigerator, so feel free to make a big batch to last you through the week.

᭞ Combine the salad ingredients in a large bowl. Add a dash of salt and 1 teaspoon olive oil. Massage the kale and cabbage to help it soften.

᭞ In a food processor, blend dressing ingredients until they are combined and smooth. Pour over salad, toss, and let marinate for 30 minutes or so before serving.

Notes:

MARINATED VEGETABLE SALAD

Serves: 8

½ cup olive oil
¼ cup white wine vinegar
1 tablespoon Italian seasoning
1 tablespoon organic Dijon mustard
1 tablespoon minced garlic
¾ teaspoon sea salt
½ teaspoon ground black pepper
3 cups cauliflower florets
2 cups cherry or grape tomatoes
1 cup bottled roasted red peppers, diced
3 medium zucchini, cut into bite-size pieces
3 carrots, cut into bite-size pieces
1 small onion, diced

Note: You can substitute different vegetables for those listed above.

꙾ In a small bowl, combine the olive oil, vinegar, Italian seasoning, Dijon mustard, garlic, salt and pepper. Whisk together.

꙾ In a large bowl, combine all of the vegetables. Pour in the marinade and toss gently, coating all of the vegetables.

꙾ Cover and refrigerate for 2 to 24 hours, stirring occasionally. The longer you marinate it, the stronger the flavor. Serve with a slotted spoon.

Notes:

MEDITERRANEAN SALAD

Serves: 4

¼ red onion, sliced

2, 15-ounce cans garbanzo beans, drained and rinsed

2 tablespoons olive oil

1½ cups marinated artichoke hearts

⅔ cup kalamata olives, pitted and chopped

2 tablespoons lemon juice

Sea salt and black pepper, to taste

🌿 Add onions, garbanzo beans and olive oil to a medium saucepan. Sauté over medium heat until heated through, stirring frequently, about 5 minutes.

🌿 Add the artichoke hearts and olives and stir a few minutes more. Remove from heat.

🌿 Add the lemon juice, salt and pepper to taste. Mix well to combine and serve.

Notes:

POMEGRANATE & GREEN APPLE MASON JAR SALAD

½ green apple, sliced
2½ cups baby spinach, packed, divided
¼ cup pomegranate seeds
¼ cup raw walnuts
¼ cup goat or feta cheese

⤷ In a wide-mouth Mason jar, layer in the following order:

- ~ Green apple
- ~ 1 cup baby spinach
- ~ Pomegranate seeds
- ~ 1 cup baby spinach
- ~ Raw walnuts
- ~ Goat or feta cheese

⤷ When you are ready eat, empty the contents of the jar onto a plate and enjoy!

Note: Spreading the baby spinach over several layers keeps the ingredients from blending too much in the jar.

Notes:

QUICK QUINOA MASON JAR SALAD

Serves: 1

½ cup black beans, drained

¼ cup of your favorite organic salsa

½ cup red quinoa (cooked according to package and cooled)

2 handfuls mixed salad greens

1 package 100-calorie guacamole*

* Note: Keep package of guacamole unopened until you are ready to eat. Packages of single-serve guacamole are usually in the produce section of your grocery store.

This Mason jar salad uses some pre-prepared ingredients, so you can throw this together in minutes!

∾ In a wide-mouth Mason jar, layer the following ingredients: beans, salsa, quinoa and greens. Place lid on top until ready to serve.

∾ When ready to serve, dump all ingredients onto a plate and top with guacamole.

Notes:

TACO MASON JAR SALAD

¼ cup fresh salsa
½ cup black beans, rinsed and drained
½ cup tomatoes, chopped
¼ cup cheddar cheese (optional)
1 tablespoon green scallions, finely chopped
½ cup ground turkey meat (cooked in home-made taco seasoning)
2 cups mixed salad greens

When you are making tacos for your family, make a little extra for your lunches the next week! This Mason jar salad will give you that on-the-go lunch needed for a busy week.

🌿 In a wide-mouth Mason jar, layer the ingredients in the order they are listed above.

🌿 When you are ready eat, empty the contents of the jar onto a plate and enjoy!

Notes:

DRESSINGS & SAUCES

AVOCADO & FETA SPREAD

Makes 1 cup

1 medium avocado
¼ cup of feta cheese
½ tablespoon fresh lemon juice
1 teaspoon extra virgin olive oil
Pinch of each: black pepper, cayenne pepper, garlic powder

꙾ Mash the avocado and feta cheese together in a bowl.

꙾ Add lemon juice, olive oil, black pepper, cayenne pepper and garlic powder mix until smooth.

This is great on a burger.

Notes:

BARBECUE SAUCE

1 cup ketchup (see recipe for homemade ketchup)

3 tablespoons raw apple cider vinegar

1 tablespoon coconut oil

1½ tablespoons black strap molasses

¼ cup maple syrup

1 tablespoon onion powder

½ tablespoon each: ground mustard, sea salt, and garlic powder

↪ In a medium saucepan, bring all ingredients to a boil. Reduce to low heat and simmer for 20 minutes, stirring occasionally.

↪ Cool and store in the refrigerator.

Notes:

CREAMY GOAT CHEESE DRESSING

Makes approximately ½ cup

4 ounces goat cheese
3 tablespoons extra virgin olive oil
1½ tablespoons raw honey
2 teaspoons raw apple cider vinegar
½ lemon, juiced
Sea salt and black pepper to taste

Place all of the ingredients in a blender or food processor and process until smooth and creamy. You may need to add extra olive oil to get the right consistency.

Notes:

HEMP SEED RANCH DRESSING

½ cup extra virgin olive oil
¼ cup lemon juice
2 tablespoons low sodium tamari
½ cup water
¼ cup shredded coconut
1 tablespoon nutritional yeast
1 cup hemp seeds
1 garlic clove
¾ teaspoon black pepper
1½ tablespoon dried dill
¼ cup loosely packed fresh cilantro leaves

◡ Place all of the ingredients in a blender and blend until smooth.

Notes:

224

KETCHUP

Makes approximately 1 cup

7-ounce container tomato paste (no additional ingredients added)

2 tablespoons raw apple cider vinegar

2 tablespoons raw honey

½ teaspoon sea salt

¼ teaspoon onion powder

⅛ teaspoon allspice

⅛ teaspoon cloves

⅛ teaspoon cayenne pepper (optional)

Up to ½ cup water

❧ Whisk together all ingredients. Slowly add water until you reach the right consistency.

❧ Refrigerate overnight to let the flavors combine.

Notes:

LEMON VINAIGRETTE SALAD DRESSING

¾ cup extra virgin olive oil

¼ cup lemon juice

¼ teaspoon sea salt

1 clove garlic, crushed

1 teaspoon organic Dijon mustard (no added sugar)

Freshly ground black pepper to taste

Optional: cayenne pepper and/or turmeric

 Combine all and shake until ingredients are thoroughly mixed.

Notes:

MAYONNAISE

Makes approximately 1½ cups

1 whole egg
2 egg yolks
¼ cup raw honey
1 tablespoon organic Dijon mustard
1 tablespoon lemon juice
1 teaspoon raw apple cider vinegar
½ teaspoon sea salt
Dash cayenne pepper (optional)
½ cup avocado oil
½ cup extra virgin olive oil

Variations:

~ Garlic, minced
~ Fresh basil, chopped
~ Tarragon
~ Fresh parsley

✎ Blend egg, egg yolks, honey, mustard, lemon juice, apple cider vinegar, salt and cayenne pepper in a food processor or high speed blender for 30 seconds.

✎ With the food processor or high-speed blender running, slowly add your oils. Start out with very small drops working up to a small stream. Blend until the consistency of mayonnaise.

Notes:

MUSTARD

½ cup mustard powder
½ cup water
Sea salt to taste

Optional additions:
~ chopped fresh parsley
~ lemon zest, and/or
~ raw apple cider vinegar

❧ Combine ingredients in a small bowl and mix well.

❧ Let stand for at least 15 minutes to let the flavors combine before serving.

Notes:

Lemon Vinaigrette Salad Dressing *page 226*

"*Each season's harvest is nature's prescription for optimal health.*"
- Dr. John Douillard

Raw Strawberry Jam *page 231*

Barbecue Sauce *page 222*

RASPBERRY VINAIGRETTE DRESSING

1 cup fresh or frozen organic raspberries, thawed

1 tablespoon organic Dijon mustard

1 teaspoon white wine vinegar

1 tablespoon extra virgin olive oil

✦ Place all of the ingredients in a blender or food processor and process until smooth and creamy.

✦ You may need to add extra olive oil to get the right consistency.

Notes:

RAW STRAWBERRY JAM

Makes approximately 1½ cups

2 tablespoons chia seeds
¼ cup warm water
4 cups strawberries (or any other berry)
2 tablespoons raw honey

↩ Soak chia seeds in warm water for 10 minutes.

↩ Blend all ingredients together and store in refrigerator.

Adapted from recipe by Patricia Murray Holcombe.

Notes:

SIMPLE WORCESTERSHIRE SAUCE

Makes approximately ¾ cup

½ cup raw apple cider vinegar

2 tablespoons water

2 tablespoons coconut aminos

¼ teaspoon each: ground ginger, mustard powder, onion powder, and garlic powder

⅛ teaspoon each: ground cinnamon and black pepper

☙ Combine all the ingredients in a small saucepan and let simmer for 4 minutes over medium-low heat.

☙ Cool and store in the refrigerator.

Notes:

SPICY BARBECUE SAUCE

Makes approximately 1½ cups

½ cup coconut amino acids

5 tablespoons pure maple syrup

7-ounce container tomato paste

3 tablespoons raw apple cider vinegar

3 tablespoons ground mustard

1 teaspoon each: onion powder, garlic powder, and sea salt

Dash black pepper

½ teaspoon cayenne pepper, optional

～ Mix all of the ingredients together in a bowl.

～ Store in the refrigerator until ready to use.

Notes:

SUPER SIMPLE SALAD DRESSING

½ cup extra virgin olive oil
2 tablespoons balsamic vinegar
1 teaspoon organic Dijon mustard
½ teaspoon raw honey
¼ teaspoon sea salt
2 tablespoons fresh parsley
Black pepper to taste

🍃 Place all of the ingredients in a clean glass jar and shake vigorously for 15 seconds.

Notes:

TAHINI SALAD DRESSING

Makes approximately 1 cup

3 tablespoons fresh lemon juice

1½ teaspoons tahini paste (or organic Dijon mustard)

3 tablespoons apple cider vinegar

3 tablespoons extra-virgin olive oil

½ cup water

Sea salt and black pepper to taste

↩ Place all of the ingredients in a blender or food processor and process until smooth and creamy.

Notes:

BALi Testimonial

"The BALi Eating Plan®...it's the real deal. BALi is not a diet with starting and ending points found on a bathroom scale; it's a healthy lifestyle that the whole family can enjoy for life. Though it's based on good, solid and sound science, you don't have be a chemist in the kitchen or scientist to understand it. It's a lifestyle that's not limited to esoteric menus and exotic ingredients. In *Simply* BALi, Jen and Dawn will positively impact lives. They explain the basic principles behind BALi in a clear and concise way. Simply BALi makes it easy and will allow you to 'take the training wheels off' and experiment with BALi on your own. The barometer of success with BALi is overall health. BALi should be part of any healthy lifestyle, and Simply BALi will help get you there."

J. Kevin Martin, D.C.,
Owner of Martin Chiropractic Health & Nutrition Center.

BREADS & MUFFINS

CHOCOLATE CHIP PUMPKIN MUFFINS

> **Makes 18 muffins**

1½ cups organic oat flour or blanched almond flour

½ cup coconut sugar (use stevia if going sugar free)

¼ cup raw honey (use another ¼ cup stevia if going sugar free)

1 teaspoon baking soda

½ teaspoon sea salt

½ cup coconut oil or grass-fed, organic butter

2 organic, free-range eggs

1 can pumpkin puree (pure raw pumpkin, not the pie mix)

1 teaspoon vanilla extract

1 teaspoon almond extract

½ cup rolled oats (not instant)

Sprinkle with ground cinnamon to taste

1 cup 70% dark chocolate mini chips or cacao nibs

꙳ Preheat oven to 325° F. Spray muffin cups with coconut oil.

꙳ Mix together dry ingredients, and set aside.

꙳ Beat eggs, add oil or butter, vanilla, almond, cinnamon, honey, and pumpkin.

꙳ Add to dry ingredients. Mix thoroughly and add chocolate chips.

꙳ Bake for 20 minutes.

Recipe contributed by Jessica Sutterfield (RealResultsFitness.net)

Notes:

COCONUT BLUEBERRY MUFFINS

1 cup almond butter
1 cup almond or coconut flour
3 organic, free-range eggs
½ cup raw honey
⅓ cup unsweetened shredded coconut
⅓ cup coconut oil, melted
½ teaspoon baking soda
½ teaspoon aluminum-free baking powder
¼ teaspoon sea salt
Pinch ground cinnamon
½ cup fresh, organic blueberries

♥ Preheat oven to 350 ° F and grease a muffin pan.

♥ Add all of the ingredients except blueberries to a medium bowl and mix until combined.

♥ Stir in blueberries.

♥ Add the batter to a muffin pan and bake for 15 to 20 minutes.

♥ Remove from pan and enjoy!

Notes:

"CORN" BREAD

Makes one 9 x 13-inch pan

6 organic, free-range eggs
¼ cup raw honey
1½ cup finely ground, blanched almond flour
½ cup grass-fed, organic butter, melted
½ teaspoon sea salt
½ teaspoon aluminum-free baking soda

Variations:

~ 1 to 2 green onions, chopped
~ ½ cup cheese
~ 2 to 3 tablespoons raw honey
~ Chopped jalapeno

This is a much healthier version of traditional cornbread.

❧ Preheat oven to 325° F. Prepare a 9 x 13-inch baking dish.

❧ In a medium bowl, whisk all ingredients together.

❧ Pour mixture into baking dish and bake for 30 to 40 minutes or until lightly browned on the top.

❧ Let cool for 15 minutes before serving.

Notes:

"A healthy outside starts from the inside."

Coconut Blueberry Muffins *page 240*

Quick & Easy BALi Breadcrumbs *page 243*

Whole Spelt Bread *page 246*

QUICK & EASY BALI BREADCRUMBS

Makes 1 cup breadcrumbs

3 slices Ezekiel or other bread
1 teaspoon Italian herbs

❧ Cut bread into cubes, place on a cookie sheet and place in low set broiler for 4 minutes, turning halfway or until golden brown.

❧ Crumble up with your hands or pulse in food processor.

❧ Mix in seasoning.

Notes:

SPELT BISCUITS

2 cups spelt flour, plus additional to flour the surface

1 teaspoon sea salt

1 tablespoon aluminum-free baking powder

6 tablespoons cold, grass-fed, organic butter, cut into small pieces

⅔ cup unsweetened almond milk

Variations:

~ **Cheese**

~ **Chives**

~ **Oregano**

~ **Onion**

ೡ Preheat oven to 450° F.

ೡ In a large bowl, combine the flour, salt and baking powder.

ೡ Use 2 knives to cut in the butter until it resembles coarse crumbs. You can also add the dry ingredients to a food processor and pulse the small pieces of butter until they resemble coarse crumbs.

ೡ Gradually stir in the milk until it forms 1 dough ball. You may need to adjust the amount of milk used.

ೡ Use additional spelt flour to flour the surface. Roll out the dough to about 1-inch thick. Cut into biscuits and place on a baking sheet.

ೡ Bake for 12 to 15 minutes, until the bottoms have become golden brown.

Notes:

SWEET CORNBREAD MUFFINS

Makes 9 muffins

1 cup finely ground, blanched almond flour
⅓ cup coconut flour
4 teaspoons aluminum-free baking powder
½ teaspoon sea salt
3 organic, free-range eggs, room temperature
2 tablespoons coconut oil, melted
½ cup unsweetened almond milk
¼ cup raw honey

Variations:
  ~ 1 to 2 green onions, chopped
  ~ ½ cup cheese
  ~ Chopped jalapeno

୶ Preheat oven to 350° F. Line a muffin pan with 9 baking cups.

୶ In a medium mixing bowl, combine the almond flour, coconut flour, baking powder and salt.

୶ In a small bowl, mix the eggs, coconut oil, almond milk and honey.

୶ Pour the wet ingredients into the dry ingredients and mix until fully combined.

୶ Pour the batter into the baking cups and bake 17 to 19 minutes or until golden brown.

୶ Let cool for 15 minutes and enjoy!

Notes:

WHOLE SPELT BREAD

2 ¼ cup room temperature filtered water, divided

2 tablespoons dry active yeast

1 to 2 tablespoons raw honey

½ cup full-fat, unsweetened, organic coconut milk

1 tablespoon sea salt

6 to 8 cups organic whole spelt flour (1 ½ to 2 pounds)

Coconut or olive oil to grease bowl and loaf pans

Recipe contributed by Terri Wilkinson, The Flour Garden (theflourgarden@gmail.com)

Notes:

√ Pour ¼ cup room temperature, filtered water into a large bowl. Add the yeast and honey. Mix and let yeast proof until bubbly.

√ Add remaining water and coconut milk.

√ Add salt and spelt flour 1 cup at a time. Stir with a wooden spoon until dough begins to form a cohesive ball and becomes too thick to stir with spoon. (Spelt flour is delicate and performs better with hand kneading rather than machine kneading.) Knead by hand in bowl or on a lightly floured surface, adding small bits of flour at a time. Lightly dust your hand with more flour to keep dough from sticking. Knead dough by turning outside edge into the middle, turn the dough a quarter turn and repeat until the dough forms a smooth ball. When dough forms a cohesive fairly smooth ball that has incorporated all the bits of dough, stop kneading. Cover dough with a clean cloth and let rest for 5 minutes while you clean the bowl and oil it with coconut or olive oil.

√ Place dough in oiled bowl, cover with cloth and let rise until doubled in bulk, approx. 1 to 1 ½ hours.

√ Punch down and let rise again for 45 minutes.

√ Punch down again and divide dough into two equal loaves. Gently press into an elongated oval and form loaf shape. Place into 2 greased, 2-pound loaf pans.

√ Let loaves rise, covered, for 30 to 45 minutes until slightly mounded over edge of pan. Do not let loaves rise too high, as they are very delicate and will finish rising in oven. When there is about 15 minutes left, preheat the oven to 350° F and arrange racks so pans can be placed in the center of the oven.

√ With a sharp thin knife, gently make a slit lengthwise down the center of dough to allow steam to escape. Bake 35 to 40 minutes until very lightly browned and loaves sound hollow when tapped. Gently remove from pans and place on rack to cool.

246

ZUCCHINI MUFFINS

Makes 6-8 muffins

1 cup flaxseed, ground
½ cup raw walnuts, ground
¾ cup BALi whey protein powder
2 teaspoons aluminum-free baking powder
1 teaspoon baking soda
1 teaspoon ground cinnamon
½ teaspoon sea salt
4 teaspoons olive oil
2 organic, free-range eggs
2 teaspoons vanilla extract
⅔ cup zucchini, peeled and grated
⅔ cup ricotta cheese
Grated zest of one orange
½ cup raw walnuts, chopped

∞ Preheat oven to 350° F.

∞ Line muffin tin with paper muffin cups.

∞ In a small bowl, mix flaxseeds, walnuts, protein powder, baking powder, baking soda, cinnamon, and salt.

∞ In a large bowl, mix oil, eggs, vanilla, grated zucchini, cheese, and orange zest.

∞ Fold dry ingredients into liquid ingredients. Fold in chopped walnuts.

∞ Pour into muffin tins and bake for 20 to 25 minutes.

Notes:

BALi Testimonial

"At 50 years old, I was struggling with my weight, having little energy and just going through the motions and accepting my decline. It is especially hard for me because I was a football player through my high school years and then worked out in the gym all my adult life.

I got in the trap of making excuses because I was working 12-hour days and claimed I did not have time to take control of my situation.

What I did not realize is that by eating better your life begins to change. You do not have to be on a "diet" or eat like a rabbit. You just have to educate yourself and make healthier choices. This is what happens when you follow the BALi Eating Plan®. You discover you can enjoy the foods that you like by changing ingredients to make them better for you.

By using the BALi Eating Plan®, it opened my eyes to a whole new lifestyle. I have been eating the BALi way for a 1½ years and have lost 60 pounds. I have more energy for work and play. I sleep better, I look better and I am a much happier person. People say I actually look younger.

One more thing that the BALi lifestyle has brought me is having fun in sharing the cooking with my wife. My wife and I search to change our once favorite family dishes to BALi-style dishes. They taste great and I know they are so much better for us. I will never go back to my old lifestyle. Special thanks for the healthier cookbook to help people heal their bodies with food."

Ron McCoon
Fresno, CA

GUILTLESS SWEET TREATS

ALMOND BUTTER POWER BALLS

Makes 20 balls

¼ cup cocoa powder

½ cup ground flaxseed

½ cup almond butter

2 tablespoons raw honey

1 tablespoon butter or ghee

Extra cocoa powder or BALi whey protein powder for rolling

❧ Mix all ingredients together. Place mixture in the refrigerator for 20 minutes for easier handling.

❧ Roll into balls and dip in cocoa powder or protein powder.

Notes:

APPLE CINNAMON DONUT HOLES

Makes 24-28 donut holes

Donuts:
⅔ cup coconut flour
½ cup coconut sugar
3 tablespoon ground cinnamon
½ teaspoon baking soda
½ teaspoon sea salt
3 large organic, free-range eggs
½ cup coconut oil or grass-fed, organic butter
1 large green apple, grated

Cinnamon Sugar Topping:
⅓ cup coconut sugar
2 tablespoons ground cinnamon
5 tablespoons coconut oil or grass-fed, organic butter

Notes:

∿ Preheat oven to 350° F.

∿ In a large bowl, combine all of the donut hole ingredients. To grate the apple, first peel the skin off using an apple peeler or knife. Then use a cheese grater to shred the apple into tiny pieces.

∿ Using your hands, pack the dough into small round balls. Be sure to pack it tight or you will have air holes in your donuts, which will make it more difficult for them to stay together. Place donut holes on a baking sheet covered with unbleached parchment paper.

∿ Bake for 15 minutes.

∿ While they are in the oven, prepare the topping by melting the coconut oil/butter in a small saucepan. Then, mix the sugar and cinnamon in a small bowl.

∿ Let the donut holes cool for 3 to 5 minutes. Dip them in the melted butter/oil and roll them in the sugar/cinnamon mixture.

∿ Let sit and enjoy!

CARROT CAKE

Makes 1 small cake

3 organic, free-range eggs
²/₃ cup melted coconut oil
¹/₃ cup raw honey
1 tablespoon vanilla extract
½ teaspoon sea salt
¹/₃ cup plus 2 tablespoons coconut flour
½ teaspoon aluminum-free baking powder
1 teaspoon ground cinnamon
½ cup shredded organic carrots (purple if possible)
½ cup organic currants

Cream Cheese Frosting
1 cup organic cream cheese (ideally grass-fed)
²/₃ cup softened, grass-fed, organic butter
¼ teaspoon vanilla extract
¼ cup powdered xylitol (powdered in a coffee bean grinder)

ↂ Preheat oven to 350° F and grease a small cake pan.

ↂ Whisk together eggs, oil, honey, vanilla and salt. Then, gradually whisk in coconut flour. Let sit for 5 minutes to thicken.

ↂ Whisk in baking powder and cinnamon.

ↂ Stir in carrots and currants.

ↂ Bake for 10 to 20 minutes in the prepared pan.

ↂ Cool completely prior to icing.

Cream Cheese Frosting

ↂ Mix ingredients together until a smooth cream is made.

ↂ Apply it to the top of the cake.

Notes:

CHOCOLATE CAKE

2 cups almond flour
¼ cup unsweetened cocoa powder
½ teaspoon sea salt
½ teaspoon baking soda
1 cup raw honey
2 large organic, free-range eggs
1 tablespoon vanilla extract

✒ Preheat oven to 350° F. Grease a 9-inch cake pan.

✒ In a medium bowl, combine the almond flour, cocoa powder, salt and baking soda.

✒ In a large bowl, combine the honey, eggs and vanilla extract. Gradually add the dry ingredients to the wet ingredients, stirring constantly until well combined.

✒ Add the batter to the greased cake pan. Bake for 35 to 40 minutes, until toothpick inserted into the center comes out clean.

✒ Let the cake cool in the pan before icing.

Notes:

254

CHOCOLATE CAKE FROSTING

Makes enough for 1 small cake

¾ cup heavy whipping cream
4 ounces 70% or higher dark chocolate nibs or chips

❧ Heat the whipping cream in a small pot over medium heat.

❧ Once the cream is hot to the touch, turn off the heat and slowly add the chips, stirring until all the chips are melted.

Notes:

CHOCOLATE CHIA MOUSSE

1 cup unsweetened almond or full-fat, unsweetened, organic coconut milk

2 tablespoons whole or ground chia seeds

¼ cup almond butter or peanut butter

2 tablespoons raw cacao powder

2 teaspoons pure maple syrup or 12 to 15 drops vanilla stevia

Optional toppings:

~ raspberries

~ strawberries.

~ Combine all ingredients in a container.

~ Cover and place in refrigerator for 30 minutes.

Notes:

CHOCOLATE CHIP COOKIES

Makes approximately 15 cookies

1½ cups almond flour
¼ teaspoon sea salt
¼ teaspoon baking soda
1 tablespoon ground flaxseed
1 tablespoon coconut flour
1 large egg
2 tablespoons coconut oil
½ teaspoon vanilla extract
¼ cup pure maple syrup
½ cup dark chocolate chips

Preheat oven to 350° F.

In a medium bowl, combine the dry ingredients.

In another bowl, thoroughly combine the wet ingredients.

Slowly fold the wet ingredients into the dry ingredients, stirring to combine. Then, stir in chocolate chips.

Let batter set in refrigerator for 30 minutes. Then, scoop out dough and roll into balls. Place cookies on parchment-lined cookie tray, and flatten for even cooking. Refrigeration isn't absolutely necessary, but cooling the dough makes it easier to handle.

Bake cookies for 12 to 15 minutes, then allow to cool for 5 minutes before moving to a cooling rack. Enjoy!

Notes:

COCONUT WHIPPED CREAM

1 can full-fat, unsweetened, organic coconut milk
2 teaspoons maple syrup (optional)
¼ to ½ teaspoon vanilla extract

Use this whipped cream just like you would regular whipped cream in desserts and frostings or over a bowl of berries. If using it for frosting, store the decorated cake or cupcakes in the refrigerator until ready to serve.

✌ Place the can of coconut milk in the refrigerator overnight. This will allow the coconut cream to separate from the liquid.

✌ Five minutes prior to preparing your coconut whipped cream, place a small mixing bowl in the refrigerator to keep everything cold while you are preparing it. Remove the chilled can from the refrigerator and flip it upside down. This will make it so that the liquid part (the part that does not thicken) is at the top of the can now.

✌ Open the can and pour the liquid into a container for use later in smoothies, baking or cooking. Scoop the coconut cream into your chilled bowl. Using a hand mixer, whip the cream until fluffy. Add the maple syrup and vanilla extract and mix it again.

Note: Consider leaving a few cans in the back of your refrigerator for a quick whipped cream. This way you always have it on hand and do not have to wait overnight.

Leftover whipped cream can be stored in the refrigerator for up to 10 days (maybe even longer) in a sealed container. Simply scoop the whipped cream into a bowl and re-whip it when you need it.

Notes:

258

DARK CHOCOLATE CHEWY BROWNIES

Makes 9-12 brownies

1½ cups black beans, drained and rinsed
½ cup rolled oats (not instant)
¼ cup almond butter or coconut oil
2 tablespoons cocoa powder
½ cup pure maple syrup or raw honey
¼ teaspoon sea salt
2 teaspoons vanilla extract
½ teaspoon aluminum-free baking powder
⅔ cup 70% dark chocolate chips (plus ¼ cup for on top)

These brownies are a crowd favorite. They are thinner than regular brownies, but they have a delicious, dark chocolate taste. They are also packed with nutrients from the black beans.

～ Preheat oven to 350° F and grease 8 x 8-inch pan.

～ Combine all ingredients, except dark chocolate chips, in a food processor and blend well.

～ Stir in ⅔ cups dark chocolate chips.

～ Pour into pan and sprinkle ¼ cup dark chocolate chips on top.

～ Bake 15 to 18 minutes, then let cool for 15 minutes prior to cutting.

Notes: _____

_____

_____

_____

DECADENT CHOCOLATE PUDDING

1 can full-fat, unsweetened, organic coconut milk

½ cup warm water

4 ounces pitted dates

½ cup raw cacao or cocoa powder

¼ cup chia seeds

1 tablespoon melted coconut oil

2 teaspoons vanilla extract

¼ teaspoon sea salt

Optional toppings:

~ coconut whipped cream
~ raspberries
~ strawberries,
~ blackberries
~ blueberries

↩ Blend together all of the ingredients in a high-speed blender until completely smooth.

↩ Pour into serving bowls, cover, refrigerate for at least 6 hours.

Notes:

JAVA CHOCOLATE CAKE

Makes one 9 x 13-inch cake

2 cups almond butter

3 tablespoons grass-fed, organic butter or ghee

½ tablespoon raw apple cider vinegar

½ tablespoon baking soda

¾ cup unsweetened applesauce

½ cup plus 2 tablespoons cacao powder

4 large organic, free-range eggs

¾ teaspoon stevia

½ cup plus 2 tablespoons coconut sugar

½ tablespoon vanilla extract

2 tablespoons cold coffee

¼ cup 70% or higher dark chocolate nibs or chips

~ Preheat oven to 325° F and grease a 9 x 13-inch baking pan (using butter/ghee or coconut oil).

~ In a medium bowl, combine the almond butter and butter/ghee. Add the apple cider vinegar and baking soda and stir until they begin to react. Add the remaining ingredients and mix until batter is smooth.

~ Pour batter into prepared pan and bake for 30 to 35 minutes or until the center is done (it is done when a toothpick placed in the center of the cake comes out clean).

~ Cool completely prior to topping with frosting.

Notes:

LACE COOKIES

4 tablespoons grass-fed, organic butter
½ cup coconut sugar
2 tablespoons organic heavy cream
⅓ cup finely chopped pistachios
¼ cup rye flour
¼ teaspoon sea salt

∝ Preheat oven to 350° F.

∝ Bring to a boil the butter, sugar and cream (approximately 1 minute). Remove from heat. Stir in the nuts, flour and salt.

∝ Drop by teaspoons onto a parchment-lined cookie pan. Note: They must be placed 4 inches apart. Bake for 4 minutes. Rotate pan and bake for an additional 4 minutes.

∝ Cool for 5 minutes and serve.

Notes:

> "Chemically speaking, chocolate really is the world's perfect food."
>
> – Michael Levine

Dark Chocolate Chewy Brownies *page 259*

Chocolate Chip Cookies *page 257*

LEMON RASPBERRY GUMMIES

¾ cup lemon juice
1 cup frozen raspberries
3 tablespoons raw honey
¼ cup grass-fed gelatin

꩜ Place lemon juice and raspberries in a blender and blend on high until completely mixed. Pour into a saucepan.

꩜ Add the honey and gelatin and whisk together. You will have a thick paste. Turn the heat on low, and continue to whisk the mixture for 5 to 10 minutes, until it becomes thin and everything is incorporated. Take off the heat.

꩜ Pour into molds or a small baking dish. Set in the refrigerator for at least 1 hour to firm up.

꩜ If you used a small baking dish, cut into bite-size squares. Otherwise, remove gummies from their molds and enjoy!

Notes:

NO-BAKE COCONUT CANDIES

Makes 20

½ cup coconut oil
½ cup cocoa powder
½ cup raw honey
2 teaspoons vanilla extract
⅛ teaspoon sea salt
1⅓ cups unsweetened coconut flakes

In a small pan, heat and whisk coconut oil, cocoa powder, honey, vanilla and salt until melted.

Add coconut flakes.

Spoon onto wax paper.

Chill in the refrigerator.

Notes:

NO-BAKE DARK CHOCOLATE & RASPBERRY PROTEIN COOKIES

Makes 18 cookies

1½ cups oat flour (rolled oats ground into a flour)

½ cup coconut flour

1 cup vanilla BALi whey protein powder

1 tablespoon stevia (optional)

½ teaspoon sea salt

½ cup plus 2 tablespoons nut butter of choice (almond butter preferred)

½ cup raw honey

¼ to ½ cup full-fat, unsweetened, organic coconut milk

Cacao nibs

Dried raspberries and cranberries (fruit juice sweetened)

Recipe contributed by Jessica Sutterfield (RealResultsFitness.net)

Notes:

_____

_____

_____

These healthy no-bake dark chocolate and raspberry cookies are refined sugar free, gluten free, vegan and high in protein! The perfect snack between meals or workouts and only requires one bowl and 5 minutes!

ℛ Line a large baking tray with parchment paper and set aside.

ℛ In a large mixing bowl, combine the oat flour, protein powder, stevia and salt and mix well.

ℛ In a small pan, add the nut butter and honey. Heat until melted and mix to incorporate.

ℛ Add the liquid mixture to the dry mixture and stir until fully combined. The mixture should be crumbly.

ℛ Slowly add milk, 1 tablespoon at a time, until a very thick dough is formed. Stir through the cacao nibs, dried raspberries and cranberries until fully incorporated.

ℛ Using your hands, form small balls and press down to a cookie shape on the baking tray. Using a fork, press down on it twice and refrigerate for at least 30 minutes before consuming. These can be stored at room temperature. If refrigerated, thaw very slightly.

PEPPERMINT BARK

Serves: 3

1 cup 70% dark chocolate chips
10 drops peppermint oil
¼ cup cacao nibs

✍ Melt 1 cup 70% chocolate chips (can use higher % if you can find).

✍ Add 10 drops of peppermint oil and cacao nibs.

✍ Pour out on wax paper and let harden. Then break into chunks and enjoy!

Recipe contributed by Jessica Sutterfield (RealResultsFitness.net)

Notes:

REFRIGERATOR CHOCOLATE

$\frac{2}{3}$ cup cocoa powder

$\frac{2}{3}$ cup warmed coconut oil or grass-fed, organic butter

$\frac{1}{3}$ cup raw honey (for a stiffer, crunchier texture, use coconut sugar)

$\frac{1}{2}$ teaspoon vanilla extract

$\frac{1}{8}$ teaspoon sea salt

$\frac{1}{2}$ cup of mixed nuts

✎ Mix all ingredients together, except the nuts.

✎ Stir in the nuts until fully combined.

✎ Pour the mixture onto wax paper, chill in the refrigerator and cut into squares.

Note: You can also sprinkle the top with a bit of salt and coconut sugar before chilling.

Notes:

SCRUMPTIOUS BROWNIES

Makes 36 mini brownies

1 cup coconut sugar
½ cup of spelt or rye flour
⅓ cup cocoa powder
¼ teaspoon aluminum-free baking powder
¼ teaspoon sea salt
2 organic, free-range eggs
½ cup extra virgin olive oil
1 teaspoon vanilla extract

❧ Preheat oven to 350° F. Prepare a 9x 9-inch pan.

❧ In a medium bowl, mix the coconut sugar, flour, cocoa powder, baking powder and salt.

❧ In another small bowl, mix together eggs, olive oil and vanilla.

❧ Pour the liquid into the dry mixture and mix well.

❧ Bake for 20 minutes.

Notes:

STRAWBERRY COCONUT ICE CREAM

Makes 2-3 servings

1 can full-fat, unsweetened, organic coconut milk

2 cups strawberries, stemmed

2 tablespoons unsweetened shredded coconut

2 tablespoons raw honey

1 tablespoon vanilla extract

꙰ Place all ingredients into a blender.

꙰ Then, pour into serving size containers. Freeze until ready to eat.

꙰ Top with optional additional strawberries.

Notes:

STRAWBERRY SMOOTHIE POPS

Makes 4-6 popsicles

1 cup sliced strawberries
½ cup raspberries
⅓ cup raw spinach (optional)
¼ to ½ cup milk or yogurt
¼ teaspoon ground cinnamon
½ teaspoon vanilla extract

✌ Combine everything in a blender or food processor until smooth.

✌ Pour into popsicle molds or paper cups, and insert spoons or popsicle sticks.

Notes:

TREASURE COOKIES

2¾ cups blanched almond flour

½ cup rolled oats (not instant)

1 teaspoon aluminum-free baking powder

½ teaspoon baking soda

⅓ cup coconut sugar

⅓ cup raw honey

1 cup grass-fed, organic butter at room temperature

2 teaspoons almond flavor

2 teaspoons vanilla extract

2 cups dark chocolate chips

2 organic, free-range eggs (at room temperature)

Notes:

↩ Preheat oven to 350° F.

↩ Mix the flour, oats, baking powder and baking soda.

↩ In a different bowl, combine the coconut sugar, honey, butter almond flavor and vanilla extract. Wait to add the eggs until after you have beaten the other wet ingredients so the eggs don't get over beaten. This keeps the cookies from getting too dense or tough.

↩ Add room-temperature eggs to the sugar/butter mixture. This helps the cookies to rise better than using cold eggs.

↩ Incorporate the dry ingredients and chocolate chips. Don't over mix, just until all the flour is mixed in. Use a large ice cream scooper and dish out onto your cookie sheet.

↩ Bake for 8 to 11 minutes. You want to pull them out when you just start to see browning on the edges.

Recipe contributed by Jessica Sutterfield (RealResultsFitness.net)

VANILLA CUPCAKES

Makes 6 cupcakes or 1 small, loaf-sized cake

¼ cup coconut flour
⅛ teaspoon sea salt
⅛ teaspoon baking soda
3 organic, free-range eggs
¼ cup coconut oil
2 tablespoons raw honey
1 tablespoon vanilla extract

Note: For chocolate version, add 1 tablespoon raw cacao powder

⤾ Preheat oven to 350° F.

⤾ Combine dry ingredients together in a small bowl.

⤾ Mix wet ingredients together in another small bowl.

⤾ Gradually add the dry ingredients to the wet ingredients, stirring constantly.

⤾ Pour into cupcake liners, filling ¾ full.

⤾ Bake for 20 to 25 minutes, until toothpick inserted into the center comes out clean.

Recipe by Amy Thedinga

Notes: _____

_____

_____

VEGAN BUTTER PECAN ICE CREAM

1 cup mixed roasted nuts (with extra pecans in the mix)

¼ cup raw honey

Pinch of ground cinnamon

1 teaspoon of vanilla extract

Add 3 to 4 cups of ice

❧ Place all ingredients into a Vitamix or Blendtec blender in the order listed and secure lid. Choose ice cream option. Blending should take no longer than 60 seconds.

❧ Stop the blender. Do not over mix or melting will occur. Serve immediately, and top with extra pecans if you wish.

Notes:

WARMING APPLE & WALNUT CRUMBLE

Serves: 4

3 apples, seeded and sliced
Juice of 1 lemon, divided
1 cup almond flour
¼ cup raw walnut pieces
¼ cup coconut oil, melted
3 tablespoons pure maple syrup
¾ teaspoon ground cinnamon, divided
2 pinches sea salt

🌿 Preheat oven to 375° F.

🌿 Place the apple slices in a 9 x 9-inch baking dish, and squeeze the juice from half of the lemon over them. Toss slightly to coat the apples in the juice and sprinkle ¼ teaspoon cinnamon on top.

🌿 In a small bowl, combine the almond flour, walnuts, coconut oil, juice from half the lemon, maple syrup, cinnamon and salt. Spread the topping evenly over the apples.

🌿 Bake until the apples are well cooked, and the top is golden brown (approximately 30 to 40 minutes).

Notes:

"Food is the most powerful medicine to heal chronic illness."

- Mark Hyman, M.D.

Chocolate Chia Mousse *page 256*

Strawberry Coconut Ice Cream *page 270*

SMOOTHIES

SMOOTHIE TIPS

Make sure to add liquids in first
because it is easier on your blender.

If you would like your smoothies to be colder,
you can add ice cubes to them prior to
blending. Just make them the last thing
you add to the blender.

Freeze fruit for a thicker consistency.
Chop it up for easier blending.

Try to "chew" your smoothie to kick start
digestive enzymes and let them know food
is coming their way!

Smoothies can also be frozen in a popsicle holder
to help alleviate a fever or sore throat.

Smoothies can both supercharge your immune system and your ability to shorten the duration of illness.

Notes:

ANTIOXIDANT-RICH RASPBERRY LEMONADE SMOOTHIE

Serves: 1

1 cup frozen raspberries**
1 cup cold water
½ cup fresh lemon juice
2 tablespoons Greek yogurt
1 to 2 tablespoons raw honey
1 teaspoon Camu Camu (optional)
¼-inch piece ginger

** *You can use BALi Purples if you do not have frozen raspberries.*

➷ In a blender, combine ingredients until smooth.

➷ Add more water if necessary to reach desired consistency.

Notes:

APPLE PIE SMOOTHIE

Serves: 1

1 cup unsweetened almond milk

1 green apple, seeded and chopped

2 tablespoons chia seeds

1 teaspoon vanilla extract

½ teaspoon ground cinnamon

½-inch piece fresh ginger

Pinch nutmeg

Pinch sea salt

Handful of almonds or 2 tablespoons almond butter

In a blender, combine ingredients until smooth.

Add more water if necessary to reach desired consistency.

Notes:

BLACKBERRY COCONUT SMOOTHIE

6 ounces water

¼ cup full-fat, unsweetened, organic coconut milk

½ to 1 cup frozen blackberries

10 raw almonds

½ teaspoon ground cinnamon

1 tablespoon ground flaxseeds

1 tablespoon grass-fed gelatin

1 serving vanilla BALi whey protein powder

≈ In a blender, combine ingredients until smooth.

≈ Add more water if necessary to reach desired consistency.

Notes:

COCOA CHIA SMOOTHIE

Serves: 1

1 tablespoon chia seeds
1 avocado
1 cup unsweetened almond milk
1 tablespoon raw cacao powder
¼ teaspoon ground cinnamon
½ teaspoon raw honey
1 large handful spinach
3 ice cubes
Optional: stevia to taste

In a blender, combine ingredients until smooth.

Add more water if necessary to reach desired consistency.

Notes:

In life, much like smoothies, you get out what you put in.

Pumpkin Spice Smoothie *page 289*

Greens Galore Smoothie *page 287*

Experiment and create your own smoothie

CRANBERRY RASPBERRY REFRESHER

Serves: 1

½ cup frozen unsweetened cranberries
1 handful spinach
½ cup frozen raspberries
1 cup almond or coconut milk
1 teaspoon coconut oil
1 tablespoon grass-fed gelatin
½ teaspoon vanilla extract
½ teaspoon ground cinnamon

🥄 In a blender, combine ingredients until smooth.

🥄 Add more water if necessary to reach desired consistency.

Notes: _____

_____

_____

_____

DARK CHERRY SMOOTHIE

Serves: 1

1 cup unsweetened almond milk
½ to 1 cup dark frozen cherries
½ cup frozen kale
½ teaspoon ground
1 tablespoon grass-fed gelatin
4 raw Brazil nuts or 6 raw almonds

Optional:
~ 3 fresh mint leaves

∾ In a blender, combine ingredients until smooth.

∾ Add more water if necessary to reach desired consistency.

Notes:

GREENS GALORE SMOOTHIE

Serves: 1

2 cups filtered water
½ cup frozen blueberries
Handful fresh spinach*
2 collard greens leaves, stemmed*
2 kale leaves, stemmed*
1 tablespoon ground flaxseeds
Ice (optional)

* You can use BALi Greens if you do not have these ingredients.

In a blender, combine ingredients until smooth.

Add more water if necessary to reach desired consistency.

Notes:

MINT BLISS SMOOTHIE

¾ cup unsweetened Greek yogurt
¼ cup fresh mint, tightly packed
1 cup unsweetened almond milk
1 tablespoon raw cacao powder
1 cup baby spinach
1 tablespoon maple syrup
1 cup ice

Optional: stevia to sweeten

In a blender, combine ingredients until smooth.

Add more water if necessary to reach desired consistency.

Notes:

PUMPKIN SPICE SMOOTHIE

Serves: 1

1 cup unsweetened almond milk
½ cup pumpkin puree
½ ripe avocado
1 teaspoon raw honey
½ teaspoon vanilla extract
¼ teaspoon ground cinnamon
⅛ teaspoon ground ginger
1 scoop BALi whey protein powder
Pinch of nutmeg, cloves, allspice

❧ In a blender, combine ingredients until smooth.

❧ Add more water if necessary to reach desired consistency.

Optional whipped topping:

Chill 1 can of full-fat coconut milk in the refrigerator overnight. Then, beat the coconut milk using a hand mixer with ½ teaspoon vanilla and 1 teaspoon honey.

Notes:

SLIM-O-NADE SMOOTHIE

Serves: 1

1 scoop BALi Greens*

1 scoop BALi Purples*

1 scoop BALi Whey*

2 tablespoons to 2 ounces black seed oil*

(Use enough black seed oil so that your appetite is suppressed)

8 to 10 ounces cold filtered water

Mix all ingredients in cold water. You can also take the black seed oil separately, if you prefer.

Slim-O-Nade Benefits
By Roby Mitchell, M.D.

You may find yourself struggling with food cravings that sabotage your efforts at sticking with the BALi Eating Plan®. This happens due to overgrowth of Candida yeast. This organism normally lives in the colon of all humans and is normally beneficial. However, as thyroid hormone and hydrochloric acid levels decline, this creates conditions conducive for overgrowth of Candida yeast.

Candida and your brain cells compete for the same food supply - sugar. Your brain monitors blood sugar to decide whether you need to eat or not. It does not monitor fat or protein. So, if Candida overgrowth causes chronically low blood sugar levels, you will have constant cravings for carbohydrates, regardless of how much fat you carry. You end up eating to feed the Candida rather than feeding your brain.

I developed Slim-O-Nade specifically to address this situation. Slim-O-Nade combines the BALi Greens, BALi Purples, BALi Whey, and black seed oil to make a meal replacement drink. Critter killers in the black seed oil, Greens and Purples bring down your Candida levels. The BALi Whey contains immune system boosting proteins that will make your immune system more efficient at killing Candida. The amino acids in the BALi Whey and the essential fats in the black seed oil will fuel the cells in the rest of your body. When you do eat, your brain will get fed rather than the Candida. Once your brain gets fed, it will turn off the hunger signals and you will automatically start to eat less.

Once you start eating less, you will produce less of the fat storage hormone insulin. When this happens, you will effortlessly lose weight. You will also develop the self control/willpower to eat the foods you know you should be eating. Simply replace one meal per day, preferably your evening meal, with Slim-O-Nade.

*Recipe contributed by Roby Mitchell, M.D. / * See Appendix A for Resources*

FRESH JUICE

FRESH JUICE

All juice recipes serve: 1

A great way to fuel your body is to juice, juice, juice. Fresh fruit and veggie juice can give your immune system a nutritional boost. Juicing allows you to take in an amount of fresh foods that you would be hard pressed to consume if not in liquid form.

Your body is able to absorb more nutrition from juiced fruits and vegetables, up to 80 percent more. Juicing predigests food and delivers nutrients straight to your body for optimal absorption.

Juicing vegetables makes consuming lots of vegetables efficient. Eating 5 pounds of vegetables a day can be difficult, but drinking 2 large vegetable juices makes it possible.

The best foods for maximizing nutrition are leafy greens (spinach, collard greens, Swiss chard, kale, mustard greens), inflammation-fighter ginger root, potassium-packed cucumbers, and antibacterial lemons.

These plant chemicals, known as phytochemicals, hold the keys to preventing/reversing cancer and heart disease, asthma, arthritis, allergies and much more.

Juicing is like exercising. Oftentimes, you may not really get excited about the thought of doing it. It takes time and effort. You wish you could reap the benefits without actually having to do it. When you do though, you FEEL FANTASTIC! Realize that you are worth the time and effort.

A juicer is required for the following recipes.

Notes:

BLOOD REJUVENATING JUICE

2 to 3 celery stalks
1 large Swiss chard leaf
1 purple carrot
1 apple
1 garlic clove
½-inch knob ginger root
½-inch knob turmeric
½ beet

CLEAN GREEN JUICE

2 to 3 celery stalks
1 small cucumber
1 kale leaf
Handful fresh parsley
½ lemon, peeled
1 green apple
1 Swiss chard leaf

DELIGHTFUL JUICE

4 purple carrots
1 green apple
1 beet
½ lime
½ lemon
2 handfuls spinach leaves
½-inch knob ginger root
½ zucchini
½-inch knob turmeric

FRESHEN UP JUICE

1 small cucumber
2 celery stalks
¼ fennel bulb
½ lime
1 green apple
1 bunch of mint
Handful spinach

Notes:

Fresh juice is an infusion of vitamins and minerals into your body.

Freshen Up Juice *page 294*

Blood Rejuvenating Juice *page 294*, Clean Green Juice *page 294*

GINGER LEMON WATER

12 ounces spring or filtered water
Juice of ½ lemon
½ inch knob of ginger root

GINGERSNAP JUICE

2 purple carrots
1 apple
½ lemon (unpeeled)
¼-inch knob ginger root
¼-inch knob turmeric

GREEN MACHINE JUICE

6 kale leaves
1 cucumber
4 celery stalks
2 green apples
½ lemon, peeled
1-inch knob ginger root

KALE BEET JUICE

1 bunch kale
½ medium beet
2 stalks celery
⅓ head red cabbage
1 green apple

Notes:

MEAN GREEN JUICE

4 kale leaves
2 apples
2 cups spinach
½ cucumber
2 celery stalks
1 medium carrot
1-inch knob ginger root

REFRESHING JUICE

3 purple carrots
1 apple
1 celery stalk
¼ cucumber
½ lemon
1 handful spinach
½ cucumber
Small handful fresh mint leaves

SALAD-TO-GO JUICE

1 celery stalk
2 tomatoes
¼ cucumber
Handful super greens
2 purple carrots
1 apple
¼-inch knob ginger
Handful ice

SUPER VEGGIE JUICE

4 tomatoes
1 large cucumber
2 celery stalks
1 red bell pepper
¼ small red onion
2 cups fresh parsley leaves and stems
1 lime
1 handful spinach

Notes: _____

_____

_____

_____

TOMATO JUICE

2 medium tomatoes
20 fresh basil leaves
1 garlic clove

BALi Testimonial

"For years I've searched for a simple healthy way to eat. I was not interested in fad diets and unhealthy portions of protein. The BALi Eating Plan® is by far the easiest and healthiest plan I have found. The recipes in *Simply* BALi are simple, delicious and best of all, the ingredients are available in my small, rural hometown. You will not be disappointed in the taste, ease, or health benefits from using this cookbook."

Dr. Amy Dunn, DNP, RN, FNPC

ELIXIRS, TEAS & OTHER DRINKS

CITRUS-FLAVORED WATER

Makes 2-quart pitcher

1 lime
1 lemon
Filtered water, plain seltzer water, club soda

  Slice lime and lemon into rounds, then cut the rounds in half.

  Add these to jar. Press and twist with a wooden spoon or muddler just enough to release some of the juices (don't pulverize the fruit into pieces).

  Fill a 2-quart pitcher or Mason jar with ice. Pour water, seltzer or club soda to the top. Stir it with a wooden spoon. Put a lid on the pitcher or Mason jar, put it in the refrigerator and let it chill.

Note: If the fruit is not organic, make sure to peel it prior to slicing. You can drink the flavored water right away, but the flavor intensifies after 1 to 2 hours. The ice at the top serves as a sieve so that you can pour the flavored water without getting fruit pieces into your glass.

Notes: _____

_____

_____

_____

COFFEE HEAVEN

16 ounces light roast, organic coffee, prepared

1 tablespoon coconut oil, coconut butter or ghee

½ tablespoon cacao powder

¼ teaspoon vanilla extract

Dash ground cinnamon

Full-fat, unsweetened, organic coconut milk to taste

Coconut sugar, xylitol, or stevia to taste (if you sweeten your coffee)

↝ Prepare coffee.

↝ Once prepared, add coffee and the remaining ingredients to a blender. Blend until completely combined. Enjoy!

Notes:

DEHYDRATION BUSTER

Serves: 1

20 ounces warm water
¼ teaspoon sea salt
1 teaspoon raw honey (optional)

☙ Add the ingredients to a glass.

☙ Stir constantly until thoroughly combined.

Notes:

DR. FITT LATTE

12 ounces light roast organic coffee

1 scoop BALi whey protein powder

¼ teaspoon ground cinnamon

2 tablespoons blackstrap molasses or raw honey

2 tablespoons black seed oil

The black seed oil makes this a very potent coffee. Keep this in mind when ready to drink.

↩ Prepare coffee.

↩ Once prepared, add coffee and the remaining ingredients to a blender. Blend until completely combined. Enjoy!

Notes:

EGGNOG

Serves: 6

2 cans original unsweetened coconut milk
½ cup almond milk
4 organic, free-range eggs
2 teaspoon vanilla
½ cup xylitol
1 teaspoon ground nutmeg
½ teaspoon ground cinnamon
⅛ teaspoon pumpkin spice
½ to 1 cup spiced rum (optional)

Combine all the ingredients, except for the spiced rum, into a blender.

Blend on high speed until froth begins to appear.

If adding spiced rum, start by adding ½ cup and slowly increase until reaching your personal liking.

Mix well.

Place in the refrigerator and chill. The colder the better.

Notes:

GET WELL SOONER ELIXIR

Makes approximately 5 quarts or 19, 8-ounce jars

1 cup fresh garlic

1 cup fresh ginger (using a grapefruit spoon works well)

1 cup fresh turmeric

1 cup red onion

1 cup raw honey (Manuka honey even better)

½ cup fresh lemon juice

½ cup black seed oil

6 cayenne peppers (wear gloves and eye protection)

6 fresh Ceylon cinnamon sticks

Raw apple cider vinegar (enough to cover all ingredients) (organic if possible)

Suggestion for using the elixir to get well:

~ **For supporting the immune system, drink 2 ounces daily.**

~ **If you are fighting an infection, Candida, fungus, drink 2 ounces 6 times per day.**

~ **It is highly suggested to cut amounts in half for children under 12 years of age.**

Notes:

_____

_____

_____

◞ Chop all the ingredients into bite-size pieces and place in a food processor or high-speed blender

◞ Fill the Mason jars ¾ of the way then cover completely with raw apple cider vinegar.

◞ Close the jars and shake vigorously to mix well.

◞ Store the jars in a dark place or on your counter-top with a brown bag over them.

◞ Gently invert them at least once a week.

◞ Let infuse for 2 to 6 months (personal preference).

◞ When you decide your elixir is ready for use, you will strain everything into a colander lined with cheesecloth. A funnel with a coffee filter works well for small batches. You can use a plate to press the moisture out of the mixture. You can also wrap the cheesecloth around the remaining mixture and squeeze the moisture out (use gloves).

◞ Use a funnel to pour the liquid into Mason jars or amber bottles.

◞ Discard the chopped vegetables immediately.

◞ This elixir will keep for months and can be used in many dishes and salad dressings, and as an immune booster. This elixir does not need to be refrigerated.

KOMBUCHA TEA BASICS

Makes ½ gallon

6 cups filtered water, divided
½ cup organic cane sugar
3 organic tea bags (green or black)
SCOBY
Grolsch bottles
White vinegar
1 cup fruit or fruit juice of your choice

Kombucha is a fizzy, fermented tea-based beverage packed with probiotics, vitamins and enzymes. The key to kombucha's existence is the live starter culture similar to a sourdough bread starter. This is referred to as a SCOBY (Symbiotic Colony of Bacteria and Yeast). This pancake-sized disc kicks off the fermentation process. You will need to get your SCOBY online, from a local business or a friend.

ᴥ Bring to boil 2 cups filtered water. Add cane sugar and stir until dissolved. Remove from heat.

ᴥ Put in 3 tea bags (green or black organic). Let steep for 20 minutes. Then add 4 more cups filtered water and with clean hands squeeze out tea bags and discard.

ᴥ When tea cools (under 85° F), pour tea in half-gallon container.

ᴥ Add SCOBY and liquid. Don't worry if it sinks.

ᴥ Cover the top with a coffee filter and secure with rubberband.

ᴥ Put the container in a corner out of the way in the kitchen and don't disturb it. It will be forming a new SCOBY on top. In about 5 to 7 days, it will be ready to drink.

Notes:

Bottling the kombucha:

⚛ Rinse each Grolsch bottle and lid with white vinegar. The easiest way is to use a plastic funnel for the first bottle and shake it up. Place the funnel on the second bottle and pour vinegar from the first one into it and over the lid. Do this with all the bottles and drain excess out.

⚛ Rinse a plastic strainer with vinegar into a bowl that will hold your SCOBY.

⚛ With clean hands that are rinsed with vinegar, lift out the SCOBY into the bowl. It's a good time to rinse any dark yeast strands off the SCOBY with vinegar.

⚛ Place any fruit/fruit juice into Grolsch bottles. As a rule of thumb, use about a $\frac{1}{2}$-inch or less in each bottle.

⚛ Strain yeast strands out of the fermented tea into a clean vessel, if desired, saving at least 1 cup fermented tea per gallon for new batch.

⚛ You can use an 8-cup glass Pyrex measuring cup with lip.

⚛ Pour fermented tea into bottles leaving about 1-inch headspace and clamp down.

⚛ After all bottles are filled, pour new cooled tea into fermenting vessel, place SCOBY on top and pour reserved fermented tea on top. Cover as before.

⚛ If your new SCOBY is at least $\frac{1}{2}$-inch thick, you can discard the old one.

Notes:

MAYAN HOT CHOCOLATE

Serves: 2

2 cups unsweetened almond milk
¼ cup raw cacao
1 heaping teaspoon ground cinnamon
Dash of cayenne pepper
3 drops of liquid stevia or raw honey to taste

Puree everything in a blender and then warm on the stove.

Optional topping: Refrigerate a can of coconut milk. This will help to separate the liquid from the thicker portion of the coconut milk. After it has been in the refrigerator for an hour, open the can. Scoop the thick coconut milk into a bowl. Save the liquid for use in another recipe or smoothie. Beat the thick coconut milk until creamy and add to the top of your hot chocolate. Enjoy!

Notes:

"Drink your tea slowly and reverently, as if it is the axis on which the world earth revolves — slowly, evenly, without rushing toward the future."

~ Thich Nhat Hanh

Citrus-Flavored Water *page 301*

Coffee Heaven *page 302*

Eggnog *page 305*

MODIFIED GOLDEN MILK

Serves: 1-2

1 can full-fat, unsweetened, organic coconut milk

1 teaspoon ground turmeric root

1 teaspoon ground Ceylon cinnamon

⅛ teaspoon each: black pepper, cayenne pepper, ground black cumin seeds,

¼ teaspoon ground ginger

1 teaspoon raw honey (optional)

☙ Blend all ingredients together in a high-speed blender. Pour ingredients into a pan and heat until hot but not boiling.

☙ Pour into a cup, add honey if desired. Enjoy.

Notes:

PROTEIN MOCHA JAVA

16 ounces light roast, organic coffee

1 tablespoon coconut oil, coconut butter or ghee

½ tablespoon blackstrap molasses

2 teaspoons cacao powder

⅛ teaspoon ground cinnamon

Full-fat, unsweetened, organic coconut milk (as desired)

1 scoop vanilla BALi whey protein powder

~ Prepare coffee.

~ Once prepared, add coffee and the remaining ingredients to a blender. Blend until completely combined. Enjoy!

Notes:

312

PUMPKIN SPICE LATTE

Serves: 2

1 cup raw milk

½ cup plain, organic pumpkin purée

1 scoop BALi whey protein powder

1 tablespoon vanilla extract

1 to 2 drops stevia

1½ teaspoon pumpkin pie spice

10 ounces strong, brewed coffee (organic, light roast)

Mix all ingredients in blender and enjoy!

Recipe contributed by Jessica Sutterfield (RealResultsFitness.net)

Notes:

TURMERIC GINGER TEA

3 slices of fresh ginger (thickness of a nickel)
3 slices of turmeric (thickness of a nickel)
¼ lemon, sliced
Hot filtered water

Optional: raw honey, to taste

Drink up to 3 times per day.

❧ Add hot water, ginger, turmeric, lemon squeezed to a mug.

❧ Cover and let steep for 15 to 20 minutes.

Notes:

How to Motivate
Yourself to Eat Healthy

Testimonials

These testimonials show tips gathered from many who have transitioned from the Standard American Diet (SAD) to choosing healthier foods.

❖ Focus not on what you're "giving up" but on what you're gaining. Widening your palate to new and healthy foods is weird at first. But it gets easier.

❖ When I crave bad food, I remind myself that it's not me craving it. It's the overgrowth of Candida that is wanting it, so it can stay alive and keep me from feeling good. Do I fail? Yes, but I keep going. It's not a race; it's not how I can do better than you. It's how can I make the best decision for my family and me TODAY.

❖ Every time I see bread products, I see Candida. Every time I see candy, I see poor immune system and sickness. Every time I see a "box" of food, I see fake food.

❖ Sadly, the foods you eat become the foods you crave. Your taste buds will reset if you stick with the foods on the BALi Food List. I struggle with cravings and sometimes lose. Pinpointing the flavor and texture you're craving is very helpful. For example, if you are craving the crunch of fried batter, then substitute that same texture with a healthier version. Celery and roasted garlic hummus, for example. Keeping snacks in the car is crucial too. I stock up on non-perishable nuts from the bulk bin, then toast some in spicy, sweet, and/or vinegary seasonings.

❖ As we journey along and continue to learn more, we continue to evaluate replacements that need to be made in our pantry. We've already made several replacements, but still have more replacements to go – little by little. One day soon we'll look up and realize we're finally eating only the foods that fuel our body best.

❖ I remember thinking the way junk food tasted to me and my emotional connection to it was more than I could conquer. And, each time I would start a new diet, I knew I would fail, so obviously I did. But last year, I decided enough was enough, and I had to change my whole lifestyle. Not for my husband or my children or even the way I looked, but because I was miserable with myself and I wanted to love me again.

❖ Cravings for sugar were super hard to overcome for the first month but not anymore. Once I started educating myself on the effects of foods on my body, it's hard not to think about that when you're making your choices. But, you have to want it for you…no one else. You have to believe that you are worth more than the junk you're putting in your mouth.

❖ Pinpoint your weaknesses. When are you straying? Do you keep food in your house that you shouldn't? Do you fail to keep healthy snacks available? Also, are you using supplements you may need? These can help quiet the cravings and hunger!

❖ I would just say that there has to be a complete shift in the mindset. My mantra today is "food is for fueling this great life that I am blessed to live." Food is now fuel to me (though that's not to say that I still don't love to eat). It's fuel for doing all of the things we have to do and

all of the things we enjoy doing! BUT, I also had to realize that it was okay to love myself enough to make an extremely drastic lifestyle change…a change that not only benefited me, but also my family. Just believe you're worth the effort! And also, identify "trigger" foods and avoid them like the plague. It's okay to say NO!

❖ Having pre-measured snack bags of nuts or veggies helps with cravings. You may not think you want that, but once you start eating the healthy snack you forget about the bad stuff you were craving.

❖ There is no miracle pep talk, no miracle speech. I was in your same position. I had no self control and could not walk away. But you know what? I matter. My advice is to slowly start transitioning to better eating. Replace the white potatoes you would normally have, with purple or orange potatoes, etc. I know it's hard, but you can do this. Give yourself a pep talk and start making changes. If you eat something you know you shouldn't, don't beat yourself up, move forward and try again.

❖ Just think meat, veggies, salad, eggs, steel cut oats, or juicing in the morning. Then, you can figure out how to bake treats with almond meal, etc. Just keep it simple with what you love on the list. Roasted chicken, crock-pot chili or soup, make a roast. Eat Greek yogurt with blueberries, sweetened with a few drops of stevia and a sprinkle of ground cinnamon. You have to love what you are eating to be satisfied! Keep apples and almond butter around for a snack, it helps to take care of a sweet tooth!

❖ Worry less about "best." Concentrate more on progress, not perfection. What's one thing you can do every day next week that you're not currently doing?

❖ We all had to start somewhere, and as we go along, we learn more and more. Don't expect yourself to be at the same place as some who have been doing this for a few years. We still don't know it all and are learning each and every day. Find a local health food store as a source for your shopping list. If you keep those veggies cleaned and bagged in the refrigerator, it will give you something to munch on instead of reaching for something processed. Over a period of time, you will be learning to train your taste buds to less salt, sugar, and processed foods. Once you do, you will absolutely love this way of eating and you will feel so much better. You will keep learning until this is second nature to you, if you don't give up.

❖ Ease yourself into it. Don't try and change everything you eat right away. Maybe have one healthy meal a day and try and conform the things you like to eat to a healthier version. It's been hard for me because I don't like a lot of veggies. I bought a juicer and a Nutribullet, they have been my lifesavers. Don't be discouraged if at first it's overwhelming. We've all been there. Some of us are still on the path to succeeding!

❖ I used to love sugar but am now getting a divorce from it. I miss flour tortillas but I'll survive. I'm not going to be a statistic.

❖ Use BALi greens, purples and whey to replace one meal each day.

Frequently Asked Questions

What and Why

There are many foods not on the BALi Food List. If you are not sure if a particular food works for you, see below for more information.

What are "BALi-approved tortillas?"

BALi-approved tortillas consist of the tortilla recipes included in this book, Ezekiel tortillas, spelt tortillas, seed-based tortillas and other tortillas made with BALi-approved flours. Check the ingredient list to confirm there is no sugar, corn syrup or agave added to the tortillas.

What is Ghee?

Ghee is clarified butter, which means that the water and milk solids (mostly proteins) have been boiled off. It is great for cooking because the fatty acids are stable at high temperatures. Ghee stimulates the production of stomach acid, increases the absorption of other nutrients, and is very supportive for acid reflux, ulcers, and other digestive complaints. Ghee is also free of casein and other milk solids. It's a healthy alternative to health-depleting vegetable oils. As a great source of healthy fats, begin incorporating it into your diet today.

Why isn't brown rice on the BALi Food List?

Brown rice is NOT on the BALi List because there are better alternatives. Black rice and red rice are much better choices.

Why is brown rice pasta on the BALi Food List?

The brown rice pasta IS on the list because there are not that many alternatives, and it is important for beginners to have transitional pasta. There are better pasta alternatives, so for those who can transition right to those better choices, do so. These better pasta alternatives are on the BALi Food List.

There are many foods not on the BALi Food List. If you are not sure if a particular food works for you, ask yourself these questions:

❖ What is its Glycemic Index?

- How dark in color is it?

- Are there added sugars?

- Does it have critter/yeast killing potential?

- What is the protein/fiber?

- Is it free of genetically modified foods (GMOs), monosodium glutamate (MSG) and food colorings?

- Is the potassium higher than sodium?

What are GMOs?

According to the Institute for Responsible Technology, "the genes from the DNA of one species are extracted and artificially forced into the genes of an unrelated plant or animal" to produce genetically modified organisms (GMOs). "The foreign genes may come from bacteria, viruses, insects, animals or even humans. Because this involves the transfer of genes, GMOs are also known as 'transgenic' organisms. This process may be called either Genetic Engineering (GE) or Genetic Modification (GM); they are one and the same."

Though there have been NO long-term studies conducted on the safety of GMOs on humans, there have been studies that show how GMO food can possibly cause long-term problems, conditions and disorders such as: digestive problems, food allergies, reproductive disorders and possibly autism. Studies have also shown organ damage, gastrointestinal and immune disorders in animals.

Can I use regular table salt?

We highly suggest you avoid buying and consuming the white table salt that we are all accustomed to buying. Table salt is so highly processed that the product we are actually buying is 97.5% sodium chloride, chemicals, MSG, aluminum and sugar. By the time the processing is complete, all of the nutritional benefits are destroyed. Today's table salt wreaks havoc on our bodies.

What is the best kind of salt to buy? Two of the best salts to buy are Celtic sea salt and Himalayan pink sea salt. They

can range in color from off-white, pink, gray and brown. Natural salts are loaded with essential trace minerals. These essential trace minerals are easily absorbed by the body and provide many health benefits.

What's the difference between smoothies and juices?

This is a question that comes up a lot. Let's look at the benefits of each and some key tips for making each. First, note that both smoothies AND juices have great benefits. They both share some of those benefits.

Those common benefits are:

❖ Both make nutrients easier to assimilate by pre-digesting the indigestible elements.

❖ Both unlock vital nutrients that may otherwise pass through us.

❖ Those nutrients come from the cellulose in the veggies, which is an insoluble fiber and part of the rigid cell-wall of the plant.

❖ The nutrients are otherwise locked away in the

rigid cell wall unless properly broken down through:

◆ sweating greens

◆ blending

◆ juicing

◆ chewing

❖ Both have a high water content – as do most raw and living fruits and vegetables.

Select Benefits of Smoothies

❖ Blending greens breaks open the hard cell walls, unlocking the minerals, chlorophyll, and enzymes.

❖ This breakdown minimizes the toll on the digestive system – it's like someone chewing your food for you but giving you all the benefits of the food itself.

❖ It makes it really easy to consume a lot more greens than we usually would or could.

❖ We get to combine them with fruits in exciting ways to hide the flavor in ways that even a child would enjoy.

❖ Note: if your smoothie is still fibrous, go ahead and chew.

Ideas for making a blended meal (smoothie) nutritionally and digestively optimal:

❖ Fruits and greens combine well together.

❖ Younger greens and tender greens tend to be less bitter if you're trying to keep the flavor sweet.

❖ Coconut, coconut oil, coconut water, ground flaxseed, chia seeds and avocado are good fats to add to help keep your blood sugar even and get you through the day.

❖ You can add ice cubes both to keep the smoothie from overheating in a high-speed blender (if you have one) and to make it really refreshing if it's hot out.

❖ You can eat your smoothie in a bowl with a spoon or drink from a glass straw (optional).

❖ Remember your smoothie or blended soup is a meal; sit and enjoy it!

Select Benefits of Fresh Juices

Some folks question the high sugar content of juices as the fiber is removed. When it comes to store-bought or bottled juices, we're in perfect agreement. But fresh-pressed green juices are a brilliant food.

Here's why:

❖ When the fiber is removed from the plant, the nutrients actually bypass the need for digestion – they're absorbed directly into the bloodstream!

❖ This is why some people think of a fresh juice as an instant transfusion of minerals. It's often used for people going through chemotherapy. It also restores necessary nutrients after an intense workout or a hydrotherapy (sauna or steam) session.

❖ By bypassing the digestive process, the body receives the nutrients and can put that energy received toward other processes; such as repair and renewal.

❖ It makes for a great way to receive some of the benefits of fasting without depleting the body.

❖ As with smoothies, but even more so, we can consume a much larger amount of greens than we could otherwise — good stuff!

❖ Beyond cleansing, combined with a diet that contains plenty of fiber from fruits, vegetables, leafy greens, whole grains, nuts and seeds, green juices are a highly beneficial addition.

Tips for juicing and optimizing the benefits of your juice:

❖ It's best to drink juice on an empty stomach.

❖ First thing in the morning is perfect.

❖ 20 minutes before consuming anything else is ideal but not necessary.

❖ Be sure to balance leafy greens with lighter greens and veggies such as cucumber, lettuce, and celery.

❖ Celery is very alkalizing (great for the blood and heart).

❖ Cucumber is very sweet.

❖ Leafy greens are potent detoxifiers.

❖ It's best, but not necessary to drink juice when it's made.

❖ Aim to drink some immediately upon waking (and making).

Good additions to include:

❖ Peeled lemon

❖ Gingerroot

Appendix

Appendix A: Resources

Health Coaching

ShineforLifeHHC.com and
GuidingYoutoWellness.com

As health coaches, Jen Harris and Dawn Corridore specialize in helping people around the country increase their energy, improve their relationship to food, lose weight, deconstruct and control cravings, and reduce their toxic load. We look forward to helping you on your health and wellness journey!

Inner Renovo

InnerRenovo.com
Facebook: Inner Renovo

Dawn Corridore and Jen Harris are the co-owners of Inner Renovo. Here you will find links to products discussed in the book. You will also find a variety of health and wellness information.

Dr. Fitt

DrFitt.com

This is the website of Roby Mitchell, M.D. It has helpful information about BALi, health articles, supplements, beauty products, etc.

Martin Chiropractic Health & Nutrition Center

MCHNC.com

Martin Chiropractic Health & Nutrition Center is in Prairieville, Louisiana. They specialize in helping you reach your specific health goals. Dr. Martin will help you recognize the problems and take action to minimize potential impacts to your health.

Essential Oils

ShineforLifeHHC.com/YL

Essential oils and plant extracts have been woven into history since the beginning of time. They are used to support the functions of the immune system, digestion, lungs, nasal passages, nervous system, joints, muscles, skin and overall wellness. The peaceful and relaxing aromas can also promote emotional well-being and restful sleep.

Exercise

RealResultsFitness.net

Jessica Sutterfield works with men and women of all ages and fitness levels. She has programs targeted for men and women, seniors needing to increase fitness for overall health and wellness, and for those looking for weight loss solutions.

Meditation and Yoga Instructor

BGall1@yahoo.com

As a Certified Hatha Yoga Teacher, Barbara Gallucci enjoys sharing ways to use yoga and meditation for stress reduction and balance. She is registered with Yoga Alliance. RYT-500 and Y4C, Yoga 4 Cancer.

Intuitive and Integrative Health, Balance Life Naturally

www.SandyConcar.com

Together we will quiet your self-talk, your doubts and release old patterns and bring these areas of your life, which feel out of balance, into alignment with the true desires you envision so you can live the life you desire for yourself.

Food Resources:

Guiltless Superfoods
GuiltlessSuperfoods.com

All Guiltless products are made from a blend of sesame, hemp, pumpkin, poppy, chia, sunflower and flaxseeds. They never use any flours, nuts, yeast, grains, gluten or unnecessary fillers in any of the baked goods. Their sweetened products include organic coconut palm sugar as the only sweetener. This is a great resource for pizza crusts, tortillas, muffins, cookies, etc.

Bragg Organic Sprinkle – 24 Herbs & Spices Seasoning

Bragg.com

This spice blend contains no additives, no preservatives and no fillers. Adds flavor to most all recipes, meals and snacks.

Mary's Gone Crackers Breadcrumbs (Original)

MarysGoneCrackers.com/
your-products/crumbs

The crumbs are very flavorful and can be used in both savory and sweet dishes, wherever you would use bread or cracker crumbs.

Local Harvest

LocalHarvest.org

Local Harvest connects people looking for good food with the farmers who produce it. The directory lists over 30,000 family farms and farmers markets, along with restaurants and grocery stores that feature local food.

Eat Wild

EatWild.com

With more than 1,400 pasture-based farms, Eat Wild's Directory of Farms is one of the most comprehensive sources for pastured foods in the United States and Canada.

Farmers Markets

USDALocalFoodDirectories.com

To better connect farmers and buyers, and enhance awareness of available local food sources, the USDA has created three new Local Food Directories for community-supported agriculture operations (CSAs), food hubs and on-farm markets by building on the popular and comprehensive National Farmers Market Directory.

Eat Well Guide

EatWellGuide.org

The Eat Well Guide is a free online directory of sustainably raised meat, poultry, dairy, and eggs from farms, stores, restaurants, inns, hotels, and online outlets in the United States and Canada.

Food Routes

FoodRoutes.org

Food Routes' "Find Good Food" map can help you connect with local farmers to find the freshest, tastiest food possible. On their interactive map, you can find a listing for local farmers, CSAs, and markets near you.

Documentaries:

Clearing the Smoke

Fat, Sick & Nearly Dead

Food Matters

Food, Inc.

Forks Over Knives

Fresh

King Corn

Processed People

Super Size Me

Sweet Remedy

The Truth About Cancer

The Truth About Cancer: A Global Quest

The World According To Monsanto

Books:

Behind the Smile,
Marie Osmond, Marcia Wilkie and Dr. Judith Moore

Food Your Miracle Medicine,
Jean Carper

From Fatigued to Fantastic,
Jacob Teitelbaum, M.D.

Natural Hormone Replacement,
Jonathan V. Wright, M.D. and John Morgenthaler

Nourishing Wisdom, A Mind Body Approach to Nutrition and Well-Being,
Marc David

Seven Weeks to Sobriety,
Joan Matthews Larson, PhD

The 7 Habits of Highly Successful People,
Stephen Covey

The Bathroom Key,
Kathryn Kassai and Kim Perelli

The Memory Book,
Harry Lorayne and Jerry Lucas

The Mood Cure,
Julia Ross, M.A.

The Slow Down Diet: Eating for Pleasure, Energy and Weight Loss,
Marc David

The Wisdom of Menopause, *Christiane Northrup, M.D.*

The Yeast Connection and Women's Health,
William G. Crook, M.D.

Type 2 Hypothyroidism,
Mark Starr, M.D.

Why Stomach Acid is Good for You,
Jonathan V. Wright, M.D. and Lane Lenard, PhD.

Appendix B: Conversion Charts

Standard Measurements

Pinch	Less than ⅛ teaspoon
Dash	⅛ teaspoon
3 teaspoons	1 tablespoon
⅛ cup	2 tablespoons
¼ cup	4 tablespoons
⅓ cup	5 tablespoons + 1 teaspoon
½ cup	8 tablespoons
¾ cup	12 tablespoons
1 cup	16 tablespoons
2 cups	1 pint
4 cups	1 quart

Dry Measurements

1 ounce		30 grams
4 ounces	¼ pound	115 grams
8 ounces	½ pound	225 grams
16 ounces	1 pound	450 grams

Liquid Measurements

1 tablespoon	½ ounce		
¼ cup (4 tablespoons)	2 ounces		
⅓ cup	2 ⅔ ounces		
½ cup	4 ounces		
⅔ cup	5⅓ ounces		
¾ cup	6 ounces		
1 cup	8 ounces		
2 cups	16 ounces	1 pint	½ liter
4 cups	32 ounces	1 quart	1 liter
8 cups	64 ounces	2 quarts	2 liters
4 quarts	128 ounces	1 gallon	3¾ liters

Appendix C: Oven Temperatures

Roasting Temperatures Guide	
Beef	Rare 125° F Medium rare 130° to 135° F Medium 135° to 140° F Well done 155° F
Poultry	Chicken breasts 160° F Chicken thighs 165° F Turkey breasts 165° F

Oven Temperature Equivalents			
Fahrenheit	Celsius	Gas mark	Terminology
275° F	135° C	1	Very Cool or Very Slow
300° F	149° C	2	Cool or Slow
325° F	163° C	3	Warm
350° F	177° C	4	Moderate
375° F	191° C	5	Moderate
400° F	204° C	6	Moderately Hot
425° F	218° C	7	Hot
450° F	232° C	8	Very Hot
475° F	246° C	9	Very Hot
500° F	260° C	10	Broiling

Index

Recipe Index

General Index

Thyroxine (T4)   71

Tortillas   32, 161, 165, 319, 321, 328

Triclosan   67

Triiodothyronine (T3)   71

TSH   63, 70

Turkey   19, 27, 103, 107, 110, 119, 128-129, 138, 151, 182, 218, 331

Turmeric   27, 39, 43

Tyrosine   71

U

Ulcerative colitis   73

V

Vegetable oil   321

Vegetables   19, 24-25, 29, 30, 36, 40, 42, 43, 47, 49, 66, 293, 323, 325

Viruses   5, 21, 58, 69, 72-73, 322

Vitamin A   50, 73

Vitamin D3   27, 63, 72

Vitamin E   31, 50

Vitamins   30-32, 73, 295, 307

W

Water   10, 13, 23, 27, 31, 40, 42, 43, 46, 52, 66-67, 70-71, 321, 323-324

Weapons of Mass Destruction   5

Weapons of Mass Reduction   27, 68, 70, 72

Weight   13, 29, 33, 54, 58, 63, 68, 70, 104, 248, 290, 327, 329

Wheat   31-32, 34

Wine   25, 28

X

Xylitol   24, 27, 38, 39, 46, 53

Y

Yeast   21, 23, 25-29, 31, 34, 73, 224, 246, 290, 307-308, 322, 328-329

Yogurt   25-26, 39, 46, 50, 103, 319

Z

Zinc   30

Resources

Book Order Form

To order your copy of *Simply* BALi, A Complete Guide to a Healthy, Whole Foods Lifestyle, please copy this page and fill out the following information.

_____
Name

_____
Address

_____

_____
City, State, Zip

_____
Phone

_____
Email

Quantity _____ x $39.99 = _____

S&H _____

NC Residents
add 4.75% sales tax _____

Order Total _____

Shipping & Handling:
$5.75 for each book

This is payable by credit card or check (made payable to Inner Renovo).

For credit cards:

Credit card number: _____

Expiration: _____

Signature: _____

Send order form to: Inner Renovo LLC, P.O. Box 966, Wake Forest, NC 27587
Email any questions to innerrenovo@gmail.com

Book Order Form (Wholesale)

To order wholesale copies of *Simply* BALi, A Complete Guide to a Healthy, Whole Foods Lifestyle, please copy this page and fill out the following information.

_____   _____
Name   Phone

_____   _____
Company Name   Email

_____   _____
Address   Resale/Tax ID

_____
City, State, Zip

_____

Submit requests for wholesale pricing to: Inner Renovo LLC, P.O. Box 966
Wake Forest, NC 27587

Email requests for wholesale pricing or any questions to: innerrenovo@gmail.com

Simply BALi

BALi Food List

(feel free to cut out and carry with you)

Notes:

_____

_____

_____

_____

BALI FOOD LIST
(* denotes antifungal/superfood)

BALi foods control your body's level of Candida (a naturally occurring yeast), aid in insulin regulation, and increase your intake of antioxidants that can inhibit free radical damage. Choose primarily fresh or frozen vegetables; organic, unpeeled fruits; low-mercury seafood; free-range poultry; grass-fed meat (without added hormones); raw nuts; beans and seeds; plant milks; organic, and raw cheese and yogurt.

Grilling/barbecuing is more likely to create chemicals that can potentially cause cancer. Marinating meat in rosemary, dark beer or red wine neutralizes this effect.

VEGETABLES & LEGUMES
Choose fresh or frozen
Acorn squash
Aduki beans
Arrowroot
Artichokes
Asparagus
Avocado
Beets
Black beans
Black radish
Bok choy
Broccoli
Brussels sprouts
*Cabbage (purple preferred)
Cactus
Carrots (purple preferred, unpeeled)
*Cauliflower (purple preferred)
Celery
*Chard (Swiss, rainbow)
Cherry tomatoes
Chives
*Cilantro
Collard greens
Cucumber
Eggplant
Endive
Fennel
Garbanzo beans
*Garlic
*Ginger
Green beans
*Green onion (scallions)
Kale (purple preferred)
Kidney beans
*Kohlrabi
*Leeks
Lentils
Lettuces (all but iceberg)
Lima beans
Mushrooms
Mustard greens
Okra
Olives
*Onions (red/purple)
Parsley
Parsnip
*Peppers (all types, hotter the better)

Pinto beans
Potatoes (purple, skin on)
Pumpkin
Radishes
Radicchio
Rhubarb
Rutabaga
Salad savoy
Shallots
*Soybeans/edamame (organic)
*Spinach
Sprouts (all types)
*Sprouts (Broccoli)
Sweet potatoes (regular or purple)
Squash (all)
Tofu
Tomatillo
Tomatoes
Turnips
Wasabi root
Yams
Yucca root
Zucchini

FRUITS & BERRIES
"Wild crafted" for best results – organic preferred – wash but don't peel – darker the better
*Acai (no added sugar)
Apples (Granny Smith, crab)
Avocados
*Blackberries
*Blueberries
Bitter melon
Boysenberries
Cherries (sour)
*Cranberries
*Coconut
*Currants (black, red)
*Elderberries
Figs
*Goji
Gooseberries
Grapefruit
Grapes (black)

Huckleberries
Key limes
Kiwi (fruit)
Kumquats
Lemons
Limes
Ligonberries
Mulberries
Oranges (blood)
Plums (black)
*Pomegranate
Prunes
Raspberries
Sea-buckthorn
Strawberries

NUTS
Raw, no salt
Almonds
Brazil nuts
Cashews
Chestnuts
Filberts
Hazelnuts
Macadamias
Pecans
Pine nuts
*Pistachios
Walnuts (black preferred)

SEEDS
Raw, no salt
Chia
*Cumin (black)
Flax
Hemp
Pumpkin
Sesame
Sunflower

FLOURS
Amaranth
Arrowroot
Artichoke
Barley
Buckwheat
Coconut
Einkorn
Kamut
Oat flour
Rye
Sorghum
Spelt
Teff

BEAN FLOURS
Black bean
Chickpea
Fava bean
Garbanzo bean
Kidney
Lentil

NUT FLOURS
Almond
Almond meal
Ground pecans
Ground walnuts

SEED FLOURS
Flaxseed (ground)
Hemp seed
Pumpkin seed flour/meal
Quinoa
Sesame seed meal
Sunflower seed meal

Baking powder (aluminum-free)
Baking soda

GRAINS & PASTA
Amaranth
Artichoke pasta
Barley
Black bean pasta
Brown rice noodles
Buckwheat
Kamut
Mung bean pasta
Non-yeasted breads
Oats-Irish/steel cut (preferred)
Oats (rolled, not instant)
Oat bran
Oatmeal
Quinoa-black, red
Quinoa pasta
Rice-black, red
Rye
Soba
Soba noodles
*Sorghum
Spelt
Spinach pasta
Sprouted grain breads/pasta
Teff

BUTTERS & OILS
Organic, raw
BUTTERS
Almond butter
Butter
Coconut butter
Ghee

OILS
Avocado
Almond
*Black seed
*Coconut
*Extra Virgin Olive Oil (EVOO)
*Fish oil
Flax
Grapeseed
*Pistachio nut
Sesame
Sunflower
Walnut

DAIRY
Organic, raw
Butter
Coconut yogurt
Ghee
Goat cheese/milk/yogurt
Kefir
Milk (raw)
Raw milk
Sour cream
Yogurt (plain)

CHEESES
Organic, raw, w/out rBGH
& antibiotics

Asiago
Blue cheese
Cheddar
Cottage cheese
Cream cheese
Feta
Goat
Mozzarella
Parmesan
Ricotta

ALTERNATIVE MILK
Almond milk (unsweetened)
Coconut milk (unsweetened)
Goat milk (unsweetened)
Hemp milk (unsweetened)

FISH / SHELLFISH
Smaller fish = less mercury
Anchovies
Cod
Crab
Halibut
Orange roughy
*Salmon (wild caught)
*Sardines
Shrimp
Trout
*Tuna
Other fish (canned, fresh)

POULTRY
Chicken (free range)
Duck (Cornish hens & others)
Eggs
Goose
Pheasant
Turkey

RED MEATS
Grass-fed, antibiotic free
Antelope
Beef
Bison
Bonsmara beef
Buffalo
Lamb
Ostrich
Pork (uncured, unsmoked)
Rabbit
Squirrel
Veal
Venison
Wild game

SAUCES/CONDIMENTS
Bragg Liquid Aminos
Bragg Herbs & Spices
Capers
Cardamon
*Cayenne pepper
Chilies
Chili powder
Chili sauce
Chinese mustard
Chipotle
*Cinnamon

Coriander
*Cumin (ground)
*Cumin (black seed)
*Curry powder
Dijon mustard
Fennel
*Garlic (fresh)
Garlic powder
Ginger
Gomasio (sea salt & seaweed)
Honey (raw, unrefined, organic)
*Kelp
Ketchup (organic, sugar-free)
*Kim chee
Lemon juice
Lime juice
Marinara sauce (sugar-free)
Miso
Mustard
Nigella (onion seed)
Nutmeg
Nutritional yeast
Olives
Onion powder
*Oregano
Pesto
Pickles
Red chili paste
*Rosemary
Sage
Salsa
*Sauerkraut
Sea salt
Sesame seed
Sriracha
Tamari
Tarragon
Tabasco
Tomato paste
*Turmeric
Vanilla
Vegenaise mayonnaise
Vinegar

SWEETENERS
Cacao
Cinnamon
Coconut palm sugar
Honey (raw, unrefined, organic)
Luo Han Guo (Lo Han)

Maple syrup (pure)
Molasses (blackstrap, organic)
Nutmeg
Stevia
Vanilla
*Xylitol
Yacon

BEVERAGES
Water
Coconut water
Water (purified/filtered)
Water (sparkling)

JUICE
Juice made from small,
dark, bitter fruits. Smoothies and
juices (more veggies than fruit).
Organic preferred.
Currant
Pomegranate
Purple carrot
Tart cherry

COFFEE (*organic)
The darker the roast, the more
processed
Light roast (preferred)

TEAS (*organic)
Black
Green
Herbal teas
Kombucha
Pau D'Arco
*White (preferred)

WEAPONS OF MASS REDUCTION
B Complex 75
Black seed oil
*Eco Thyro (Recommend an evaluation
before taking)
IodoRX
Magnesium gel
Selenium
Vitamin D3

Simply BALi

Basic Pantry Staples

(feel free to cut out and carry with you)

Notes:

BASIC PANTRY STAPLES

- ☐ Almond butter (no added sugar)
- ☐ Almond flour
- ☐ Almonds, raw
- ☐ Apple cider vinegar, raw
- ☐ Arrowroot powder
- ☐ Baking powder, aluminum-free
- ☐ BALi whey protein powder
- ☐ Balsamic vinegar
- ☐ Basil, dried
- ☐ Bay leaves
- ☐ Black beans
- ☐ Blackberries, frozen
- ☐ Black pepper
- ☐ Blackstrap molasses
- ☐ Blueberries, frozen
- ☐ Brazil nuts
- ☐ Cacao powder, raw
- ☐ Cayenne powder
- ☐ Chia seeds
- ☐ Chicken broth
- ☐ Chili powder
- ☐ Cilantro, dried
- ☐ Cinnamon, ground
- ☐ Cocoa powder
- ☐ Coconut aminos
- ☐ Coconut flakes, unsweetened
- ☐ Coconut flour
- ☐ Coconut milk, full-fat, unsweetened, organic
- ☐ Coconut oil, unrefined
- ☐ Coconut palm sugar
- ☐ Cooking spray, coconut oil

- ☐ Coriander powder
- ☐ Cumin powder
- ☐ Currants, dried
- ☐ Curry powder
- ☐ Diced tomatoes in a jar
- ☐ Dijon mustard, organic
- ☐ Dill weed
- ☐ Dried cranberries, juice-sweetened
- ☐ Flaxseeds, ground
- ☐ Garbanzo beans
- ☐ Garlic powder
- ☐ Ghee
- ☐ Ginger root
- ☐ Grapeseed oil
- ☐ Hazelnuts, raw
- ☐ Hemp seeds
- ☐ Honey, raw
- ☐ Italian seasoning
- ☐ Kidney beans
- ☐ Lentils
- ☐ Maple syrup, pure
- ☐ Mustard powder
- ☐ Nutmeg, ground
- ☐ Oats, rolled (not instant)
- ☐ Oats, steel cut
- ☐ Olive oil, extra virgin
- ☐ Onion powder
- ☐ Oregano, dried
- ☐ Paprika
- ☐ Parsley, dried
- ☐ Pasta – brown rice, quinoa, mung bean and/or black bean pasta

- ☐ Pecans, raw
- ☐ Pinto beans
- ☐ Pistachios
- ☐ Pumpkins seeds, raw
- ☐ Quinoa (black, red)
- ☐ Red pepper flakes
- ☐ Rice, black
- ☐ Rice, red
- ☐ Rosemary, dried
- ☐ Sage powder
- ☐ Salmon, wild Alaskan canned
- ☐ Salsa
- ☐ Sea salt, Himalayan pink or Celtic
- ☐ Seasoning, Bragg Organic 24 Herbs & Spices Seasoning
- ☐ Sesame seed oil
- ☐ Spaghetti sauce in a jar, without added sugar
- ☐ Spelt flour
- ☐ Spinach, frozen
- ☐ Stevia
- ☐ Strawberries, frozen
- ☐ Tamari soy sauce
- ☐ Thyme
- ☐ Tomato paste, in a jar preferred
- ☐ Turmeric powder
- ☐ Vanilla extract
- ☐ Vegetable broth
- ☐ Walnuts, black preferred
- ☐ Xanthan gum
- ☐ Xylitol
- ☐ Yogurt, Greek plain

Other Staples

- ☐ Blackberries, frozen
- ☐ Blueberries, frozen
- ☐ Spinach, frozen
- ☐ Strawberries, frozen

Notes:

Simply BALi

Guide to Fats & Oils

(feel free to cut out and carry with you)

Notes:

_____

_____

_____

GUIDE TO FATS & OILS

Choosing the right fats and oils is essential to a healthy mind and body. Here is a guide to help you make the best decisions.

HEALTHY, Naturally Occurring Oils:

Fats for HOT uses:
~ Coconut oil (organic, unrefined)
~ Butter (pasture-raised, grass-fed, organic)
~ Ghee (pasture-raised, grass-fed, organic)
~ Lard (pasture-raised, grass-fed, organic pork fat)
~ Tallow (pasture-raised, grass-fed, organic beef fat)

Fats for LOW OR NO HEAT:
~ Olive oil (organic, extra-virgin)
~ Sesame oil
~ Macadamia nut oil
~ Avocado oil
~ Walnut oil

Fats for COLD USES:
~ Flaxseed oil
~ Hemp oil

UNHEALTHY OILS:

Trans-fats or hydrogenated oils should be REMOVED from the diet COMPLETELY. Trans-fats are created in an industrial process that adds hydrogen to liquid vegetable oils to make them more solid. The primary dietary source for trans-fats in processed food is "partially hydrogenated oils." Trans-fats are easy and inexpensive for companies to use. The oils with trans-fats can be used many times in commercial fryers. Trans-fats also raise unhealthy LDL cholesterol (increasing inflammation) and lowers healthy HDL cholesterol (good cholesterol).

AVOID:
~ Canola oil
~ Corn oil
~ Margarine/buttery spreads
~ Partially hydrogenated oils in packaged foods
~ Safflower oil
~ Soybean oil
~ Sunflower oil
~ Vegetable oil

Reference::
heart.org/HEARTORG/GettingHealthy/ FatsAndOils/Fats101/Trans-Fats_UCM_301120_Article.jsp#.Vjv2KYR1dZ8

Simply BALi

The Many Names of Sugar

(feel free to cut out and carry with you)

Notes:

THE MANY NAMES OF SUGAR

Sugar is sugar. The goal is to reduce your consumption of it. If you use sweeteners, choose sweeteners from the BALi Food List.

Agave nectar
Agave syrup
All-natural evaporated cane juice
Apple butter
Apple sugar
Apple syrup
Arenga sugar
Barley malt
Barley malt syrup
Bar sugar
Berry sugar
Beet molasses
Beet sugar
Beet syrup
Blackstrap molasses
Blonde coconut sugar
Brown rice syrup
Brown sugar
Buttered syrup
Cane crystals
Cane juice
Cane juice crystals
Cane juice powder
Cane sugar
Caramel
Carob syrup
Chicory syrup
Chocolate syrup
Coarse sugar
Coconut palm sugar
Coconut sap sugar
Coconut sugar
Coconut syrup
Coco sugar
Coco sap sugar
Concentrate juice
Concord grape juice concentrate
Confectioners sugar
Corn sugar
Corn syrup

Corn syrup solids
Corn sweetener
Cornsweet 90
Creamed honey
Crystal dextrose
Crystalline fructose
Crystallized organic cane juice
Dark brown sugar
Dark molasses
Date sugar
Decorating sugar
Dehydrated sugar cane juice
Demerara sugar
Dextran
Dextrose
D-fructose
D-fructofuranose
Diastatic malt
Diatase
D-mannose
Dried evaporated organic cane juice
D-xylose
Evaporated organic cane juice
Evaporated corn sweetener
Ethyl maltol
Florida crystals
Free flowing brown sugar
Fructose
Fructose crystals
Fructose sweetener
Fruit fructose
Fruit juice
Fruit juice concentrate
Fruit sugar
Fruit syrup
Galactose
Glucose
Glucose-fructose syrup
Glucose solids
Glucosweet

Gluctose fructose
Golden molasses
Golden sugar
Golden syrup
Gomme syrup
Granulated fructose
Granulated sugar
Granulated sugar cane juice
Grape sugar
Grape juice concentrate
Gur
HFCS
High dextrose glucose syrup
High fructose corn syrup
High fructose maize syrup
High maltose corn syrup
Hydrogenated starch
Hydrogenated starch hydrosylate
Hydrolyzed corn starch
Honey
Honey powder
Icing sugar
Inulin
Invert sugar
Inverted sugar syrup
Invert syrup
Icing sugar
Isoglucose
Isomalt
Isomaltotriose
Isosweet
Jaggery
Karo syrup
Lactitol
Lactose
Levulose
Light brown sugar
Light molasses
Liquid dextrose
Liquid fructose

Liquid fructose syrup
Liquid honey
Liquid maltodextrin
Liquid sucrose
Liquid sugar
Maize syrup
Malt
Malted barley syrup
Malted corn syrup
Malted corn and barley syrup
Malted barley
Maltitol
Maltitol syrup
Malitsorb
Maltisweet
Maltodextrin
Maltose
Maltotriitol
Maltotriose
Maltotriulose
Malt syrup
Mannitol
Maple sugar
Maple syrup
Molasses
Monosaccharide
Muscovado sugar
Mycose
Mylose
Organic agave syrup
Organic brown rice syrup
Organic cane juice crystals
Organic coconut palm sugar
Organic palm sugar
Organic sucanat
Organic sugar
Organic raw sugar
Palm sugar
Palm syrup
Panela

Pancake syrup
Panocha
Pearl sugar
Piloncillo
Potato maltodextrine
Powdered sugar
Pure cane syrup
Pure sugar spun
Raisin syrup
Rapadura
Raw agave syrup
Raw sugar
Refiner's syrup
Rice maltodextrine
Rice syrup
Rice syrup solids
Rock sugar
Saccharose
Simple syrup
Soluble corn fiber
Sorbitol
Sorbitol syrup
Sorghum
Sorghum molasses
Sorghum syrup
Sucanat
Sucrose
Sucrosweet
Sugar
Sugar beet syrup
Sugar beet crystals
Sugar cane juice
Sugar cane natural
Sulfured molasses
Super fine sugar
Sweetened condensed milk
Sweet sorghum syrup
Syrup
Table sugar
Tagatose

Tapioca syrup
Treacle
Trehalose
Tremalose
Trisaccharides
Turbinado sugar
Unrefined sugar
Unsulphured molasses
White crystal sugar
White grape juice concentrate
White refined sugar
White sugar
Xylose
Yellow sugar

Simply BALi

Notes:

Simply BALi

A Guide to Labels
(feel free to cut out and carry with you)

Notes:

A GUIDE TO LABELS

Cage Free – The animals were not put in cages. However, this does not mean they were free-range or even set foot outdoors.

Barn Roaming – These animals were not caged, but were also not free to go outside.

Free Range or Free Roaming – The animals had access to the outdoors, but this does not necessarily mean they ever went outside.

Grass-fed – Ruminant animals (cows, goats, sheep) were fed a diet of only grass and forage. Animals were able to graze.

Vegetarian-fed – Animals were not fed any animal byproduct, but may have had a diet that included grains.

Certified Humane – Animals were kept so as to allow free movement, without tethers, cages, or crates. Does not necessarily indicate access to outdoors. This label contains no information about the animals' diet.

Natural – May not contain any artificial ingredient or added color and can only be minimally processed (meaning the product cannot be fundamentally altered).

No Hormones Administered – With beef, this means no hormones were administered to the cattle. Use of hormones in raising pigs or poultry is illegal nationwide.

No Antibiotics Added – No antibiotics were used at all (even for illness) in the raising of the animals.

Certified Organic – Animals had access to bedding and the outdoors, but it's uncertain for how long. No hormones or antibiotics were used in their raising.

There are other labels that can be quite confusing because they don't have legal definitions like "sustainable" or "pasteurized."

The best place to buy your meat and eggs is at a farmers market where you can talk directly with the person who raised the animals.

Simply BALi

The BALi Lifestyle

(feel free to cut out and carry with you)

Notes:

THE BALi LIFESTYLE

In order to be healthy, we must be in balance. This includes diet, exercise, sleep, stress management, relationships, self-care, healthy elimination, sex and gratitude. Together these fuel the energy in our lives. If any one of these areas is out of balance, we often search for other ways to satisfy those needs. Many people use comfort foods. Think about where you stand in each of these areas now and use the pages here as a journal.

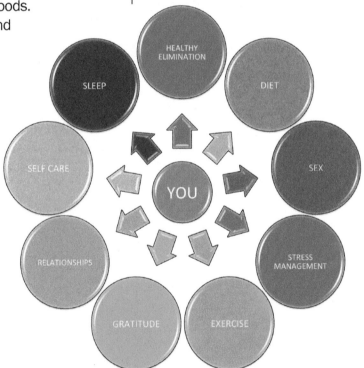

Diet

What changes do I need to make? How will I make them?

_____

_____

_____

_____

Exercise

How will I incorporate exercise on a daily basis?

_____

_____

_____

_____

Sleep

How will I improve my sleep habits today?

_____

_____

_____

_____

Relationships

How will I improve my relationships?

_____

_____

_____

_____

Stress Management/Emotional Wellbeing

What are my biggest stressors?

1 _____

2 _____

3 _____

4 _____

5 _____

6 _____

7 _____

8 _____

How will I cope with them?

_____

_____

_____

_____

Self-Care

How will I take better care of myself?

_____

_____

_____

_____

Healthy Elimination

What will I incorporate to improve my elimination?

_____

_____

_____

_____

Sex

How will I improve my sex life?

_____

_____

_____

_____

Gratitude

What am I thankful for?

1 _____

2 _____

3 _____

4 _____

5 _____

6 _____

7 _____

8 _____

Remember, I need to be grateful for every day!

Simply BALi

Notes:
_____
_____
_____
_____

CPSIA information can be obtained
at www.ICGtesting.com
Printed in the USA
LVOW06s2226030616

491120LV00030B/148/P

9 780997 027501